PICTURE OF THE WEEK

DO YOU REMEMBER THE MILK BAR?

Reader Pete Colman has sent us this photograph from 1961 of the Milk Bar, which was located on Market Place South. Looking to the right, you can see the two buildings next to the town hall which were later replaced by the current NatWest bank building.
● If you have an old photograph of the Ripon area you would like us to consider publishing, email it as a jpeg file to news@ripongazette.co.uk

Gazette 8/5/14

NOSTALGIA

Gazette 5/6/14

Milk Bar memories of Ripon

After seeing the photo recently of the Milk Bar, *pictured right*, it brought back memories to me.

In the late 1950s I worked in the Westminster Bank (now the Skipton Building Society) and remember it was the Kendrew family that ran the very busy Milk Bar.

The beautiful building next to it housed the National Provincial Bank and the tobacconists run by the Kennedys.

This building was replaced in the 60s by the National Westminster Bank building as it now is.

In the 50s the bank managers both lived in flats above their respective banks. On the other side of the town hall was the Lawrence shop, cafe, restaurant and the magnificent ballroom. Then: the Yorkshire Penny Bank; A Maynards sweet shop; George Bells outfitters; Whitelocks fruit and veg; The Wakeman's House.

I cannot remember what the building, since demolished, on the corner of High Skellgate was. Can anyone help?

Peter Benson
Roecliffe Park, Roecliffe

AN ILLUSTRATED HISTORY OF

RIPON

To the memory of my parents who would have been surprised to see my name in print; to my wife, Dorothy, children and grandchildren who have supported and encouraged me; and to the citizens of Ripon, past and present, whose story this is.

Maurice H Taylor

Acknowledgements

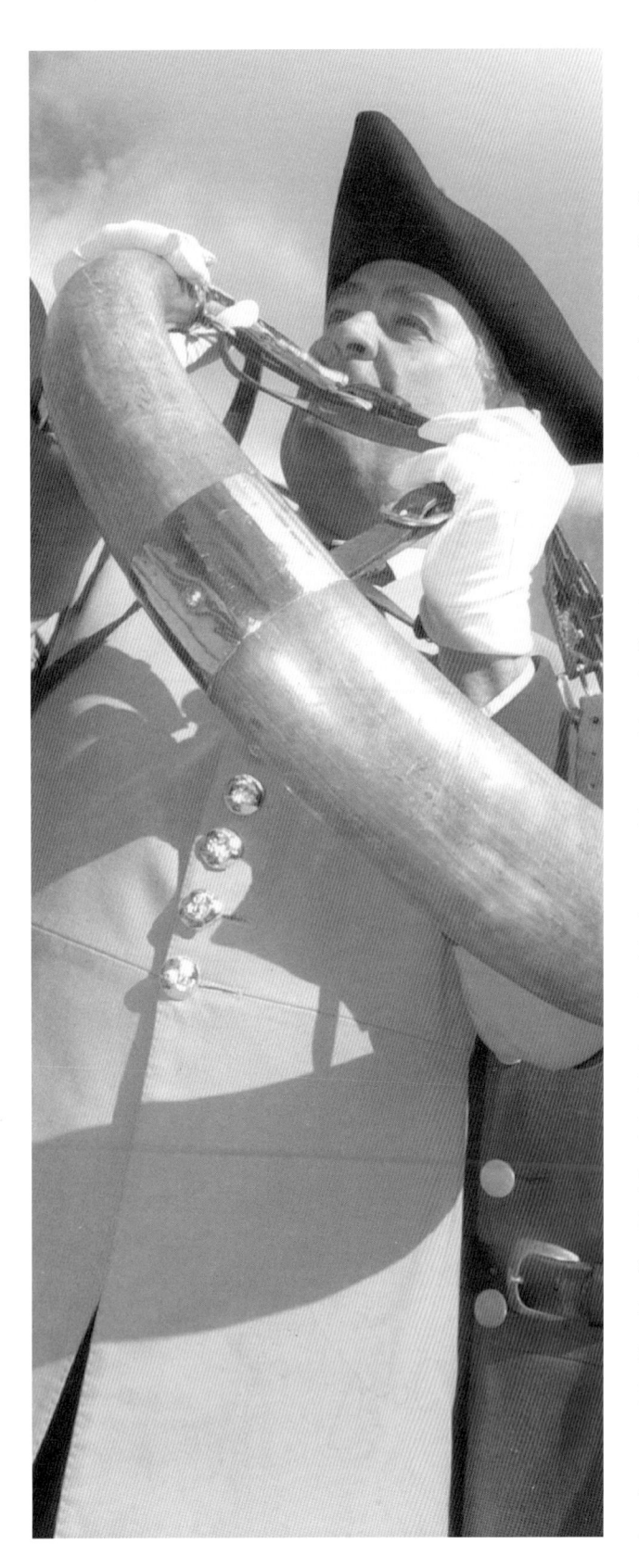

I should like to express my thanks to the following: My wife, Dorothy, for her support and encouragement. The cathedral dean and chapter for access to their library and for permission to photograph, and to the staff for much help and co-operation. Dean John Methuen; Canon Keith Punshon; Mark Punshon; Jean Denton; David Beeken; Andrew Curtis; John Hebden and Ripon Historical Society; Anthony Chadwick; Ted Pearson; Dr John Whitehead; Dr Bill Forster; Mike Younge; Peter McNamara; Beryl Thompson; Dr Bill Petchey; Mary Mauchline; Prof Glan Jones; Jean Potts; Beechey Jarratt; Mary Kershaw and David Rhodes, Harrogate Borough Council; John and Susie Wimpress; staff of Ripon Library; University College of Ripon and York St. John; Ripon Bowling Club; Mike Barlow and Ripon City Band; Mike Ridsdale, John Clarke, Ripon Swimming Club; Brian Carroll; Alan Stride; Alan Turtle; Dr Richard Hall and York Archaelogical Trust; Joy Calvert; Ron Darwin; Richard Willis; Violet Waterworth; Maurice Forth; Tom Walters; John Harrison; Mark Richards; Angus Rands; Ted Rose; Mrs Tinsley; Ripon Civic Society; James Coulson and Roy Waite, Ripon Morris Dancers; Jim Jackson; Ripon Tennis Club; Avril Hardaker; Bessie Chapman; Rev Derek Ching; and Keith Watson for additional colour and black-and-white photography; my evening class students who, by their interest and questions, have pushed me to investigate areas I thought I knew about but found I didn't, and the many unnamed friends and colleagues whose help and interest has kept me going through the project. Especial thanks to David Lee for indexing.

Maurice H Taylor
September 2005

Contents

Early days	3
'The very place where the market stede…'	6
Monastery, Minster, Cathedral	20
The growing township	46
All in a day's work	60
Civic pride	72
Fun & games	78
Back to school	96
Heroes and villains	104
Modern times	112
Notes	132
Endnote numbers	133
Appendix 1: Maps & Plans	141
Appendix 2: Street Names	142
Appendix 3: Market Place Facts	143
Appendix 4: Bibliography	145
Appendix 5: Mayors of Ripon	147
Appendix 6: Bishops of Ripon	152
Appendix 7: Members of Parliament for Ripon	153
Appendix 8: Wakemen of Ripon	158
Appendix 9: Picture credits	162
Index	164

A 9th century styca found on the site of the new Cathedral School in 2001. A horde of coins, possibly buried in the 860s was found at Ailcey Hill in 1695.

Early days

Ripon's origins can most easily be seen at Quarry Moor where, some 230 million years ago, on the edge of the tropical Zechstein sea, Ripon formed the beach, several miles wide, similar to beaches around the States of Oman.[1] Negligible rainfall meant that low tides were only about a sixth of the height of those around our coasts today and probably only reached the top of the beach during spring. To the west was a great barren desert. When the upper rocks were formed, the sea had begun to dry up and became very salty. The calcium sulphate crystals formed into layers. Hundreds of thousands of years later the layers dissolved, creating 'sink-holes' which continue to appear on the surface today.

When the Wensleydale glacier was blocked, a relatively recent 14,000 years ago, the meltwater broke through over-flow channels and came down Skeldale. Later a moraine barrage upstream of Fountains Abbey broke, its floodwater scouring out the valley and depositing debris in the plain below.

Axe heads and flints survive from the tribes who peopled the area between 4000BC and 2000BC. A 'beaker' burial of a powerfully built young man was discovered in the gravel quarry at West Tanfield in 1973.[2] To the north and east of Ripon, Neolithic henges, earth circles and Bronze Age barrows, the biggest group in the country, indicate the settlement of Celts from around 1800BC. Outside a ditch are banks from where spectators could watch the ceremonies. Flint arrow heads, human bones and funeral ashes have been unearthed nearby.

At Thornborough are three henges - large, banked and ditched, circular enclosures, equally spaced and aligned northwest to south-east, 600 yards (550m) apart. Recent excavations have shown the central henge to have been built over an earlier cursus - a long, cigar-shaped, ditched enclosure, nearly one and a quarter miles (2km) long. The concentration of monuments of this type is claimed to be unparalleled in Britain.[3]

In 1915 a sword dated to the second or third century BC, the 'Clotherholme sword', was discovered during the construction of the army camp[4]. There is a note that, in April 1960, Ripon's 'anthropoidal' sword - so called because of the shape of its hilt - returned to the city after renovation by the Tolson Museum, Huddersfield.[5]

Evidence for Romans in Ripon is sparse despite two Roman roads passing within a few miles, and it has long been suggested that there may be an undiscovered Roman site at Ripon. Following the 1997 excavations at the cathedral, Dr Richard Hall described the crypt in the cathedral, with its re-used Roman stones, as the oldest post-Roman vault to survive in England, and suggested that the builders could *'conceivably have re-used a pre-existing Roman vault'*.[6] Traditionally a Roman ford crossed the river about fifty yards (45m) below North Bridge; some coins were discovered in 1827 at Skellbank; pottery was found at North Terrace in 1866; and Walbran reported a small funeral vase having been found on the west side of North Street.[7]

In 1994 this rare iron-age sword was found near Ripon. An iron-age fort, said to be the most southerly in the country, is currently under investigation at Scotton Banks, Knaresborough.

Early days

Excavations in 1986-7 at Ailcey Hill uncovered forty to sixty burials, aged from very young to about fifty years of age. Seven were over five feet ten inches tall (180cm), and two over six feet two inches (188cm). The burial ground was in use from the sixth to ninth centuries.[11]

Also in North Street, during the demolition of property in 1852, some Roman tiles and a piece of Roman glass were found in the foundations.[8] In 1850, two peat diggers unearthed the preserved body of a man wearing a toga on Grewelthorpe Moor. Two pigs of Roman lead were discovered on Hayshaw Moor; and at Castle Dykes, near North Stainley, the burnt remains of a Roman 'camp, station or fortified villa', excavated in the 1860s, produced two skeletons, one with an arrow wound in his skull. At Well a section of Roman tiles is displayed in the church, and other Roman buildings have been identified there, including a possible swimming pool. There was a Roman villa at Sutton and a camp at Nutwith. Mosaic tiles found at these sites, or at Aldborough near Boroughbridge, may link with tiles in St. Mary Magdalen's Chapel.

We can trace the name 'Ripon' to the eighth century. In one book, by Eddius Stephanus about AD 715, it is shown as '(in)Hrypis'- the settlement of the Hrype tribe - and in another, by Bede about AD 730, as 'Inhrypum' - the monastery.[9] Other versions of the name include Hripis, Hrypsaetna, Onhripum, Rypum, Hyropan, Ripum, Ripun and Rippon.[10] The double 'p' went out of use around 1800.

Overflows from the glaciers left three silty mounds. Two survive: one on which the cathedral stands; the other, Ailcey Hill. The Skell and the Laver followed their courses to meet the Ure from Wensleydale. After the Angles landed on the East Coast, Hrype's tribe probably made its way upriver and were settled in the area by the sixth century.

Some experts say that the name Skell comes from the Celtic esk for 'water' with kell the Scandinavian for 'spring'. Others trace it to the Old Norse for 'resounding'. Its roots are the same as Ax-, Exe-, and Usk-, meaning 'to gush forth'.[12] Despite its short length the Laver was a very hard-worked mill river. Its name goes back to an ancient Celtic word meaning 'brook'. Flowing through Wensleydale, the only major dale in Yorkshire not named after its river, 'Ure' may come from the Old British 'Isura'. Spelt variously Ior/Eor/Jor/Yor in the twelfth century, the spelling had settled as Ure 'strong river', or 'holy river'[13], by the 1530s. At the start of the next century, after many years of doubt, it was decided that the River Ure would form the boundary between the North and West Ridings.

Geologically, two rock formations - magnesian limestone and new red sandstone - converge at Ripon, and it is where the Pennine Hills meet the Vale of York: in economic terms, where the shepherds meet the farmers and a market is created.[15]

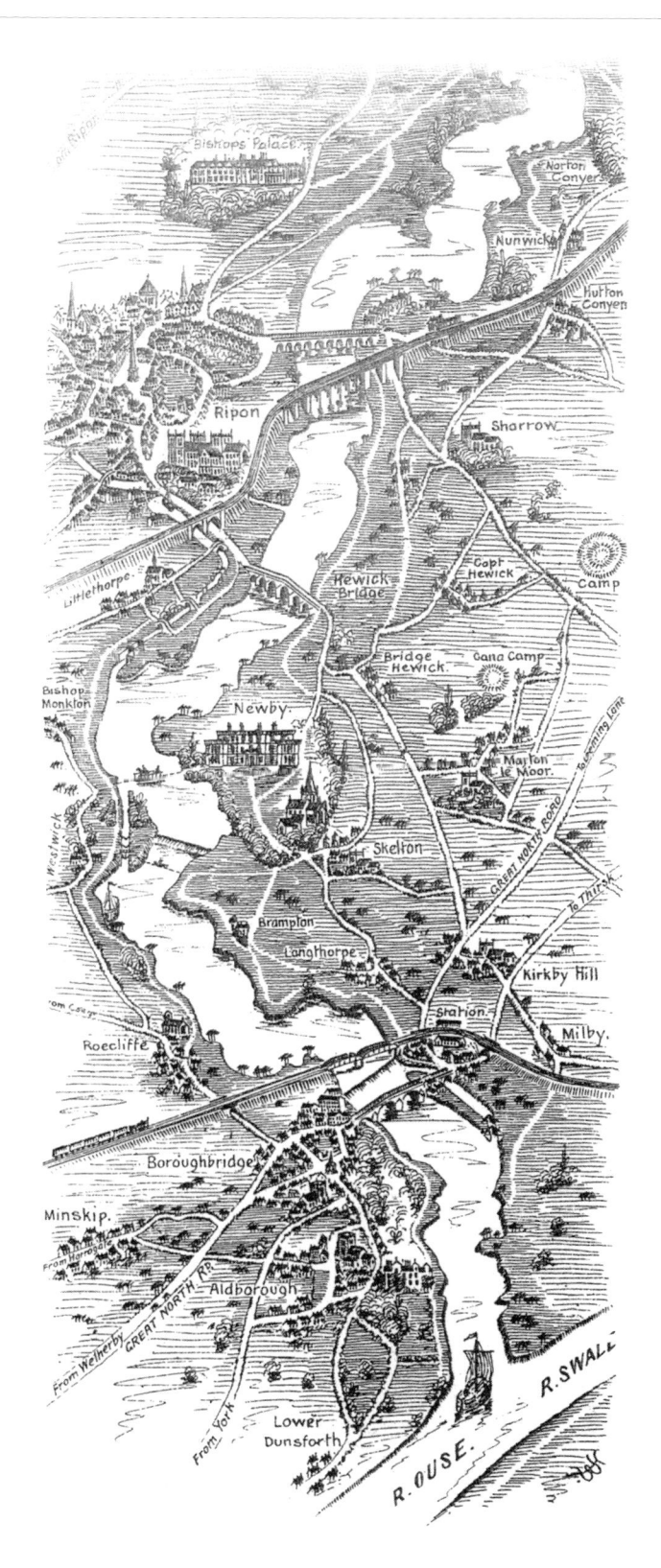

Bird's eye view of the Ure, 1891 (detail).[14]

'The very place where the market stede...'

It is likely that Ripon market had grown up long before it was granted a charter and market tolls were extracted, possibly as early as the tenth century[16] when Yorkshire was renowned for the number of its fairs and markets.

Is there any significance in the development of Thursday as Ripon's market day? Saint Wilfrid's monastery at Ripon cherished his memory. Ripon was the first of his monasteries and his principal shrine.[17] It was believed that Wilfrid had died on a Thursday and so, at the monastery, each Thursday was kept 'as a feast as though it were a Sunday'. There is little doubt that Thursdays would draw extra pilgrims to the town and traders would be quick to respond. The inspiration for Thursday as Ripon's market day can therefore reasonably be claimed to go back to the eighth century. However, it has to be said that during a trial in 1228 the canons claimed that, as well as a five-day fair for St. Wilfrid's Feast in October, since Athelstan's time they had held the right to a Wednesday market, later suppressed by the archbishop of York.

A charter, said to have been given in 1108 by Henry I to 'Thomas, Archbishop of York, and St. Wilfrid', refers to a weekly market, and a fair in April lasting the two days before the feast of St. Wilfrid, the day of the feast and the day after.[18] Certainly by 1129 Archbishop Thurstan had obtained from Henry I a grant to St. Wilfrid and the archbishopric of a four-day fair at the April feast of St. Wilfrid.[19] Such a grant was a valuable privilege.

The earliest reference to a Borough in Ripon that has so far emerged is in the Pipe Roll for 1194, which records the half-yearly fee of some £36.13s.4d being paid for 'Ripon within the borough'. In 1197 the burgesses owed £10 for having their freedom.

By the end of the thirteenth century, as well as the weekly chartered market, the fair was being held in May with another in October, but the town was feeling competition from Boroughbridge market, and from new toll-free markets at Masham on Fridays and Wednesdays.

The current view that there was no formal market in Ripon until the time of Archbishop Walter de Gray (1215-1240) is well put forward by Dr Petchey. In the early thirteenth century, on 'the largest area high enough above the rivers to be well drained ground, sufficiently level that traders' carts would not slide away', what we now know as Ripon Market Place was laid out - burgage plots (a 'toft') with a dwelling for a freeman who paid a customary rent to the Lord of the Manor, the archbishop.

In 1898 this statue of St. Wilfrid was first placed in its niche on the Knaresborough and Claro Bank, since rebuilt as the National Westminster Bank.

By the sixteenth century there were 202½ burgages, mostly paying an annual rent of four pence each, with frontages of approximately fifteen or thirty feet wide, or in the measurement of the time 8 ells (45 inches) - the standard burgage frontage in the north of England.

Before 'Le Marketstede' was laid out, where would the weekly market have been held? Old Market Place has been suggested,[20] so called by 1377, spreading across to Allhallowgate. Also likely is that buying and selling would take place around and even inside the Minster.

Despite an order of 1268 forbidding the setting out of stalls and the sale of goods in churches, some forty years afterwards Archbishop Greenfield wrote to object that the nave of Ripon Minster was being used as a common market where 'deceptions, frauds and perjuries' were committed. Trading, however, continued until the Reformation.

The south aisle has a flat-topped tomb called the Lion, or Irish tomb, on which merchants are said to have struck their bargains. At the Reformation, the church was forbidden to 'exact collections', but continued to be allowed to take tolls.

'The very place where the market stede…'

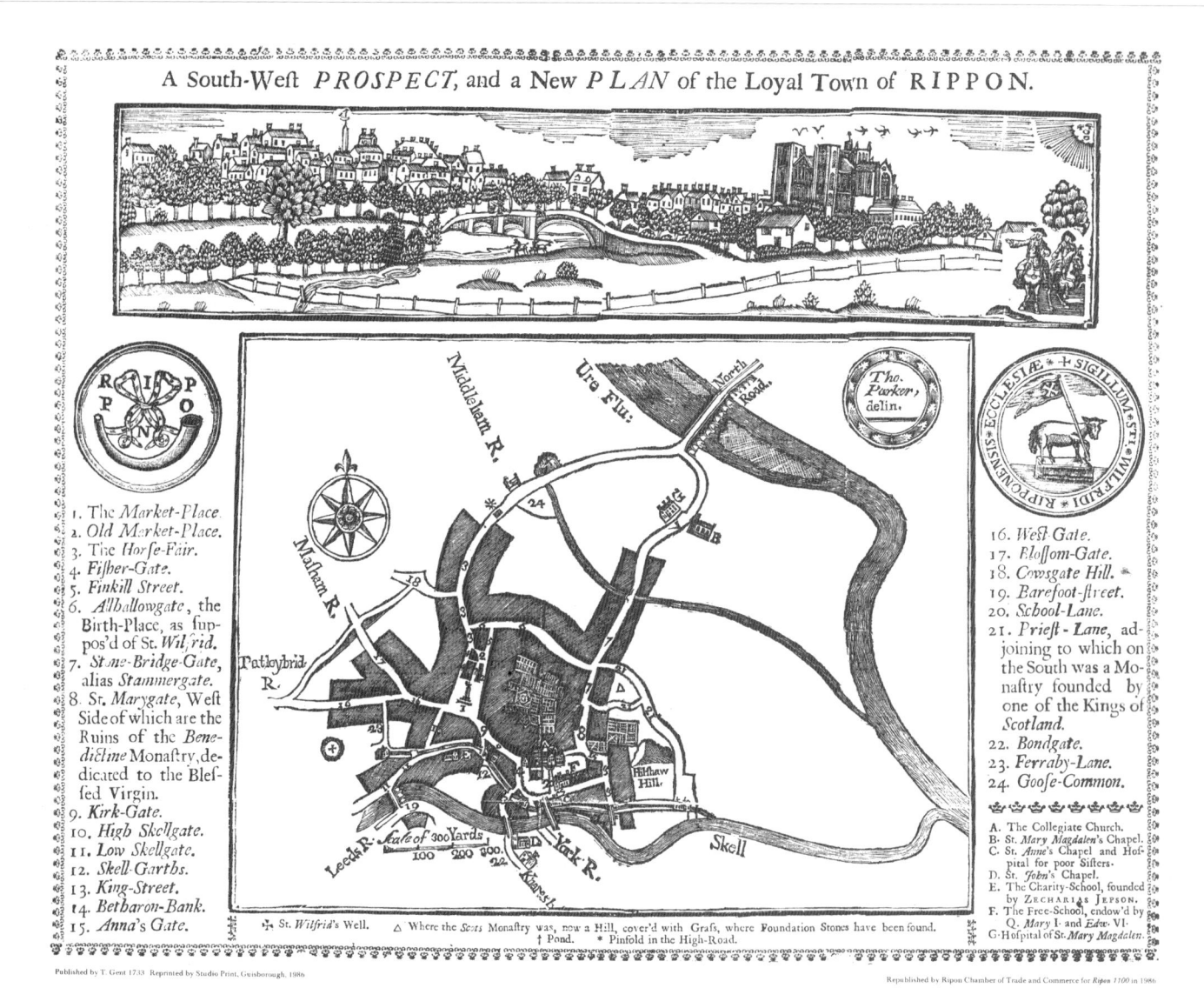

A South-West PROSPECT, and a New PLAN of the Loyal Town of RIPPON.

1. The Market-Place.
2. Old Market-Place.
3. The Horse-Fair.
4. Fisher-Gate.
5. Finkill Street.
6. Alhallowgate, the Birth-Place, as suppos'd of St. Wilfrid.
7. Stone-Bridge-Gate, alias Stammergate.
8. St. Marygate, West Side of which are the Ruins of the Benedictine Monastry, dedicated to the Blessed Virgin.
9. Kirk-Gate.
10. High Skellgate.
11. Low Skellgate.
12. Skell-Garths.
13. King-Street.
14. Betharon-Bank.
15. Anna's Gate.
16. West-Gate.
17. Blossom-Gate.
18. Cowsgate Hill.
19. Barefoot-street.
20. School-Lane.
21. Priest-Lane, adjoining to which on the South was a Monastry founded by one of the Kings of Scotland.
22. Bondgate.
23. Ferraby-Lane.
24. Goose-Common.

A. The Collegiate Church.
B. St. Mary Magdalen's Chapel.
C. St. Anne's Chapel and Hospital for poor Sisters.
D. St. John's Chapel.
E. The Charity-School, founded by Zecharias Jepson.
F. The Free-School, endow'd by Q. Mary I. and Edw. VI.
G. Hospital of St. Mary Magdalen.

St. Wilfrid's Well. △ Where the Scots Monastry was, now a Hill, cover'd with Grafs, where Foundation Stones have been found. † Pond. * Pinfold in the High-Road.

Published by T. Gent 1733. Reprinted by Studio Print, Guisborough, 1986.   Republished by Ripon Chamber of Trade and Commerce for Ripon 1100 in 1986.

There were many disputes between the archbishop, his neighbours and the canons of the Minster over their respective rights. By May 1441, hostility had been brewing for some years. The men of the Forest of Knaresborough claimed that, as tenants of the king, they were exempt from tolls at Ripon market. The archbishop brought in 300 heavily armed soldiers. Trouble flared. Soldiers and foresters chased each other across the country. At Thornton Bridge two of the archbishop's men were killed, three maimed, sixteen grievously beaten and others taken for ransom. The foresters' casualties are less clearly reported. It has been suggested that stances taken by northern magnates against the inadequacy of Henry VI and in support of the archbishop at that time, led up to the Wars of the Roses.

In deciding to lay out the market place, the archbishop was obviously seeking to increase his income. Wilfrid's new shrine would attract pilgrims to the Minster. Visits by the archbishop and his stewards drew those seeking justice, charters and religious rites. They needed food, lodging, stabling and so on, as did the archbishop's entourage and his mercenaries. If there was trading in the Minster as well as in the new market place, how many markets were there? There were certainly the corn market and 'fairs' for the sale of cloth, cattle, sheep and horses at different times of the year. The archbishop's authority set out to guarantee safety and fair trade. His officers tasted the ale, checked weights and measures, and controlled the sale of goods. The court of 'pie-powder' settled disputes and punished offenders. The name, corrupted from the French 'pieds-poudreux' meaning dusty feet, reflected the manner in which those involved appeared before the court.

It has been suggested that the market place, now some 115 yards by 82 yards (105m x 75m), originally covered an area 200 yards by 100 yards (183m x 91.5m), with Lavender Alley being more or less in the middle.[21] By the sixteenth century:

'The very place where the Market stede and the Hartt of the Towne is was sumtyme caullid Holly Hill of holy trees there growing'.[22]

Possibly from the late thirteenth century, property crept forward onto the 'square', especially noticeable on the western side, where it is suggested that the route from High Skellgate continued straight ahead, without the present 'dog-leg' junction. The tollbooth, where tolls were collected by the archbishop's officers, probably stood in the middle with the Market Cross (hence Crossgate - now Lavender Alley). At times the corporation met in the tollbooth, so it was referred to as the Towne House: the Towne Book was corrected and amended' there in 1598. Soon afterwards the tollbooth was rebuilt, but it does not seem to have survived the erection of the Obelisk in 1702.[23]

In the tollbooth 'garth', or yard, was the market cross, standing on a stone pavement, roofed to shelter the Corn Market held there, described in a deed of 1280 as 'the great cross in the market place'.

A stone cross was removed in 1611 'from the place where it stood 16 feet'. Celia Fiennes described the scene in 1698:

'... Ripon, a pretty little market town mostly built of stone, a large market place, with a high cross of several stepps: we were there the market day where provisions are very plentiful and cheape ...

Notwithstanding this plenty, some of ye inns are very dear to strangers that they can impose on.'[24]

Near to the market cross was the common bakehouse, and close by were the stocks, pillory, whipping post and gibbet. In 1786, Thomas Iveson was whipped for burning heather on Bishopside Moor, and in 1845 five lads were sitting in the stocks, three hours each, 'for gambling etc. on the Sabbath day'.[25] In 1946 four skeletons were unearthed at Gallows Hill, thought to be from the executions carried out there between the sixteenth and eighteenth centuries. 'The fatal tree stood on elevated ground near Hungry Hill. The place is yet called Gallows Hill'.[26] The last execution in Ripon of a woman, Ann Houghton, was in 1604 and of a man in 1721, after which the condemned were taken to York for execution. In 1723 the gallows were removed.

As part of the Rising of the North - the rebellion in support of the Catholic Mary against Queen Elizabeth I, which began in November 1569 - Richard Norton and Thomas Markenfield mustered troops in the market place and held a mass at the Minster. Two months later a reported 300 of their supporters from the West Riding, and 'lastly, within sight of their neighbours and homes, the misguided townsmen of Ripon', were executed. As a result of the rebellion, a heavy price was exacted in damage to the Minster, and even more damage followed in 1575 when the 'gilden tabernacle' was ordered to be demolished.[27]

'The very place where the market stede...'

During the Civil War the Puritan army under Sir Thomas Mauleverer entered the town, defaced memorials and broke windows in the Minster. Whether or not the Puritans were responsible for all the damage blamed on them, the date '1673' in nails on the west doors of the cathedral suggests that eventually new doors were needed. A detachment of Royalists from Skipton Castle, led by Sir John Mallorie of Studley Royal and *'assisted by several Ripon champions'*, surprised the Puritans in the market place and *'made them feel the sharpness of their swords'*.

In Ripon, as elsewhere in the medieval period, timber-framed buildings would have lined the streets. There is a reference to 'shoppys' in Kirkgate in 1349, the time of the Black Death, The typical pattern would be for each long, narrow plot to be occupied by a house and workshop.[28] Narrow frontages, often about fifteen feet (5m) wide, permitted the maximum number of plots around a market place or village green. In some market towns, it is said that this was to provide premises for each different trade. As time went by, two or more plots might be combined. At the back would be the kitchens, other service rooms, a garden, possibly a well and a cesspit. Later the upper storeys were jettied out over the lower ones, and later still the yard behind was filled with dwellings. This reached an insanitary peak during the population explosion of the nineteenth century, with outbreaks of cholera and typhoid in the overcrowded 'courts', as they were called.

To the east of the present town hall stood a re-fronted house and shop, formerly known as Capper Hall, which may have been the site of a medieval cloth hall. Beside it, a road ran down across a bridge over the millrace on Water Skellgate,[29] down a lane beside Jepson's Hospital (now City Club) to a ford across the river. Traditionally this is the area where the clothworkers were concentrated, and where newly woven cloth would be 'tentered', ie stretched into shape. Capper Hall carried a datestone of 1708, and was the last open-fronted shop in Ripon.

After the Reformation, local justices began to take responsibility for law and order from the manorial courts. In 1604 by the 'exertions' of the Wakeman, Hugh Ripley, who became the first mayor, Ripon obtained a charter of incorporation from James I, which permitted local government under a mayor, twelve aldermen and twenty-four councillors. A recorder, town clerk and two 'serjeants at mace' were appointed[30] and a fortnightly court of record (petty sessions) was permitted for offences up to £50, with the mayor, his two predecessors and the recorder acting as justices. This court of record appears not to have met, probably because the mayor and his predecessors sat separately as the borough court, where they dealt with minor offences and vagrants, issuing penalties such as a whipping, or time in the stocks.

It is sometimes asked if the James I charter survived the 'Glorious Revolution'. In 1686, soon after he came to the throne, James II demanded the surrender of town charters. Only after coercion did Ripon comply and another charter was issued, the changes being largely in the oaths of allegiance and supremacy demanded. Two fairs a year were granted (on the Mondays before the 20th March, and the 1st August and on the three days following), with a court of pie powder. Tolls, passage and stallage rights were reserved to the archbishop. Because of its late surrender, Ripon's 1604 charter was void.

AN ILLUSTRATED HISTORY OF RIPON

The mayor in procession, 1733. The horn was carried before the mayor by his sergeant on various 'Horn Days': Candlemas, Easter Monday, Wednesday in Rogation Week, St. Wilfrid's Sunday and St. Stephen's Day.
It is still paraded when the mayor walks formally from the town hall to the cathedral.

'The very place where the market stede...'

However, normality was restored, and a charter by James II was declared valid, by proclamation, on the 17th October 1688.[38] Problems over the oaths demanded and other difficulties followed James's abdication, and boroughs that had been at odds with the parliament of the day had their charters re-confirmed in 1690, in Ripon's case; the 1604 charter.

In the years that followed the granting of the 1604 charter, giving Ripon the status of 'Borough' and the authority to manage its own affairs, there are reports of conflicts over exorbitant tolls, disputed ownership and quarrels with neighbouring towns over rights. In 1629, the corporation minutes record impoverishment in the town 'especially by Godes late visitacion'. Plague and the loss of the two great cloth fairs worth at least £200 a year compounded the poverty, and it was agreed to establish a poor rate. The archbishop offered his ruinous palace to the corporation as a poorhouse. The corporation declined the offer, and appealed to him to set up a fulling mill.

Possibly to compensate for the loss of cloth making, lace production was introduced around 1600. Wool fairs were encouraged, although it took two years before the following resolution came into effect:

'Ordered that four public fairs for the sale of wool shall be holden during the present year [1837] in the Old Market Place - or wool market, and on the following [Thurs]days...'

Important as sheep were to the area,[31] Ripon's agricultural economy had been more widely based. Journeying through the country as Inspector of Libraries for Henry VIII, John Leland wrote:

'The faire about the fest of Seint Wilfride at Ripon is much celebraytyd for byenge of horses and cattel'.

Stray animals were impounded in the pinfold (pound), which stood on Horsefair (North Street), beyond Brewster Terrace. It is remembered in the name of some houses nearby called Pinfold Close. Along the straight stretch of Horse Lane, or Horsefair, the horses could show their paces. Ripon horse fairs date from the thirteenth century. Marmaduke Rawley wrote in his 1664 diary that he *'went to Rippon, a faire towne. It hath a very large market place where there is twice a year a greate horse faire.'*

To combat the risk of fires, the appearance of market towns like Ripon altered about this time. First, brick became acceptable, then fashionable. Some builders thought timber helped to strengthen the walls, so some timber 'strengthening' persisted into the nineteenth century. A number of medieval timber-framed buildings survive and others were rebuilt or given new façades, but by 1842 there were no thatched roofs left in the city[32] and by then the tollbooth and its market cross had long gone.

In 1702, under a scheme designed by Nicholas Hawksmoor, echoing an entire Roman-style paved forum and including a new pillory, Ripon acquired the earliest free-standing monumental obelisk in the country.[33] To finance the building of the Obelisk, Mayor John Aislabie drew on a £50 legacy from a previous mayor, William Gibson, together with contributions from churchmen and gentry. The plinth was to be 'set rough ... to keep idle persons from making letters and writing what they please upon it, and doing other Mischieves and Brutalities', but within ten years it needed repairs costing £564 11s 9d.[34]

The Market Cross or Obelisk from Gent's History of Ripon 1733.

When Daniel Defoe visited in 1726, he said that Ripon's market square was *'The finest and most beautiful square that is to be seen of its kind in England'*.
The date of 1781 on the plaque commemorates the restoration and re-modelling of the Obelisk, to celebrate sixty years as the longest-serving Member of Parliament by William Aislabie, John's son. The corporation added the plaque in 1785, and an account of 1798 tells us that the 'Obelisk being in a ruinous condition, was taken down and a new one erected, superior to the former, at the sole expense of the late William Aislabie, Esquire'. The claim that this second obelisk was superior to the original may be a reference to the erection of the four smaller obelisks, which appear on early nineteenth century illustrations.[35]

'The very place where the market stede...'

Tudor hornblower. Each night, at the four corners of the obelisk, the ceremony of Setting the Watch was peformed, after which the citizens were to remain in their houses till four or five in the morning. The tradition, now unique in England, is still performed at nine o'clock each evening at the obelisk and afterwards at the house of the mayor.

The wakeman, or watchman, also referred to as the vigilarius, is associated from medieval, or even earlier, times with the blowing of a horn, indicating the setting of the watch or curfew - a practice common across medieval Europe. The earliest evidence for Ripon's wakeman is in the fourteenth century, when wakemen are mentioned as officers of the Minster, rather than the town.[36] Originally it may well have been the wakemen's task to blow the horn themselves, but as his status grew to become that of leading citizen, a separate hornblower was appointed.

The wakeman was elected annually from the twenty-four aldermen. He regulated the markets, was responsible for the fields and commons, the town bull ('...*from henceforth the Wakeman for the time being shall not sell, kill, nor put away the town bull without the consent of the house upon pain of £10*'),[37] and looked after law and order under the archbishop's stewards.

There are presently five horns; the: charter horn; reserve horn (1690); 1865 horn, bought by the then mayor and currently in use; 1886 millenary horn - from the Chillingham herd; 1986 festival horn.

Before 1604, after the watch had been set, the wakeman could be required to compensate victims burgled during the watch - until three or four in the morning. The townspeople were required to pay him two pence for each street door, thus providing a compensation fund and paying his staff: hornblower, four byelaw graves (constables), pinder (impounded stray beasts), neatherd (cattleherd) and swineherd.[39]

14

Visiting Ripon, John Byng, Lord Torrington, recorded in his journal for the 8th June 1792:

'At 10 o'clock I repair'd to the Minster where [their] service was going to begin; but as there was no chaunting to day, I fancied it too damp; so only walk'd around the inside, where I saw some few old defaced monuments.

I enquired much about the Horn - by which the Charter is held, but in vain. At last I found out the Worshipful the mayor's house; his old wife (in manners and words a Mrs Trulliber [the wife of a character in Fielding's Joseph Andrews, a fat clergyman, ignorant, selfish and slothful] bawl's out to his worship that a stranger wanted to speak to him. Down came Mr Mayor and sent for the Horn which is nightly blown before the Mayor's house: he then enter'd into a larned and most elaborate discourse about the country, Fountains Abbey, &c, to the wonder of his wife, but to my questions could give no answer -viz as to the meeting of the English and Scotch Commissioners here in 1639, &c &c &c.

At last, the maid return'd with the Horn, a common cowherd's horn. "I'll be hang'd", cries Mrs Trulliber, "if the gentleman does not want to see our fine horn upstairs, which is allways worn on grand days". "Why, to be sure, that must be it", exclaimed Mr Mayor. So down it was brought, richly ornamented with silver, and cased in velvet; appendant to it hang a silver cross-bow, and a spur (for the making of which this town was formerly famous) with several silver plates of some of the Mayor's Arms fix'd upon a blue velvet shoulder belt. "Your arms, my dear", cried Mrs T, "should be upon 't." "Hold thy tongue", answer'd Mr Mayor; "the woman's a fule". Having seen this, I was contented, and bowed away.' [40]

The obelisk or market cross with four small, stone crosses which were replaced in 1882 by six Brays lamps around the square. Detail of etching c.1895 from a painting by Julius Caesar Ibbetson, who died in 1817, aged 58 years.

Until 1848, when a toll on corn known as the 'market sweepings' was abolished, the bellman announced the opening of the cornmarket at midday. Now he rings at the general market at eleven o'clock on Thursdays. The office is sometimes said to date from the 1604 charter but it can be dated to at least the fourteenth century. In 1367, the vicars of the minster received rents from a property in the Cornhill, next to the common bakehouse, subject to making annual payments of fourpence to the church bellringer and twopence to the town bellman. Certainly in 1668 the corporation paid for cloth for his new coat and in 1673, as town crier, the corporation *did order the bellman to tinckle the bell throughout the towne*. The old quarter sessions began with the crier calling: *'Oyez, Oyez, Oyez. All manner of persons who have anything to do at the General Quarter Sessions draw near and give your attendance'*.

His other duties included administering whippings, cleaning the market place, posting up notices, lighting fires for corporation meetings and acting as their courier. If there was likely to be a breach of the byelaws, the corporation would send the bellman to cry 'Cautions!' In 1802 it was *'ordered that the bellman's fees for making calls in the town in future be threepence each, and four-pence for the country'*.[41]

From 1533, the wakeman was entitled to stallage (a fee) at fairs, and also to dues called 'hand lawe' or 'market sweepings', at the cornmarket, of a two-hundredth part of each bushel carried into the market, later doubled. It was unpopular and difficult to collect, and in 1619 orders were given that it might be taken forcibly, though not 'riotously'.

'The very place where the market stede…'

Despite byelaws against selling corn 'by sample' - ie bringing into the market and therefore paying tax on only the small sample quantity - the practice so reduced the value of the toll that it was not worth collecting, and it was discontinued in 1848.

The black-and-white house in the south-west corner of the market place has become mistakenly associated with Hugh Ripley and called the 'Wakeman's House'. At his death in 1637, Hugh Ripley owned at least six houses in Ripon, but this was not one of them.[42] From evidence in his will, it is thought that he lived immediately to the west of the site of the town hall. But the 'Wakeman's House' is interesting even without its wakeman connection. A double-winged late medieval Tudor hall-house, with a passage entry from the market square, it is one of the few timber-framed buildings with wattle-and-daub infill to remain in Ripon. About 1600 it was reoriented to face the square. Inside are a Victorian cupboard bed, a musicians' gallery and a bolthole. By the early twentieth century, the house was in a poor condition and the council proposed its demolition, but Mayor William Hemsworth determined that the city should own and care for it, and in 1917 persuaded the city council to buy it for £1,200. After restoration the building served as a local history museum until 1954. From 1962-78 it was a tea-room, then to 1987 the tourist information office, and from 1990 it was occupied by the Ripon Improvement Trust, The building which stood at the rear for most of the twentieth century, and served for a long time as a museum, was originally built as a soup kitchen during the First World War, but never used as such. It was demolished in 2000 to make way for new public toilets.

The Wakeman's House about 1900.

'The very place where the market stede…'

Under the 1604 charter, responsibilities increased for the mayor and corporation. They occupied themselves, for example, by making sure that *'no foreyner doe kill oxen or sell flesh within this towne excepting on the Markitt Day or other days to be allowed'*; they provided *'a pair of scales and proper weights'* for weighing gold; they ordered the constables to collect *'due proportion'* from each person towards the £5 cost of repairing the highway and to see that the householders swept the streets in front of their houses.[43]

It is to Mrs Elizabeth Allanson, William Aislabie's daughter, that we owe the present town hall, built as an assembly rooms in 1799-1801 and designed by the fashionable architect James Wyatt, who was also responsible for the Drury Lane Theatre. The stone was dug from a quarry on the Studley Estate.[44] The clock was added in 1859. The suggestion for an inscription on the building may go back to 1802, when Sophia Lawrence, who later inherited the Studley Estates from her aunt, Elizabeth Allanson, wrote to the town clerk, Peter Taylor: *'I mentioned the inscription you proposed on the town hall to Mrs Allanson, but she wishes it may not take place'*.

Some eighty years later, in 1886, the text 'Except the Lord keep the city, the Wakeman waketh in vain' was inscribed on the town hall as a permanent memorial of the Millenary Festival held that year. The Ripon Millenary book refers to the motto (from Psalm 127, altering 'watchman' to Wakeman') as medieval. It has been suggested that there seems to be no evidence of its use before a sub-committee consisting of the mayor, the dean and the Rev W C Lukis, a noted local antiquary, proposed it as the inscription of a medallion struck to commemorate the 1886 Millenary Festival.[45] Without knowing the inscription proposed by Peter Taylor, it is perhaps worth recalling that the shield on the mayor's chain, dated 1859, carries not only the illustration of a spur but also the motto 'Except the Lord keep the City, the Wakeman waketh in vain'.

On the 9th November 1896, the marquis of Ripon, on his last day as mayor of Ripon, wrote to the incoming mayor:

'I am sorry to say I have a sharp chill and am confined to my bed. It will therefore be impossible for me to attend the Council to-day to offer you my congratulations on your election. It has for some time seemed to me an anomaly that the Town hall of Ripon should belong to a private individual and not the Corporation. I have discussed the matter with Lord de Grey and we have determined to make a free gift of the Town hall site and buildings to the Corporation, if they are willing to accept it. Please read this to the Council meeting to-day.'

The formal conveyance took place on the 31st July that year - Wilfrid Saturday.

Horses were sold in the Horsefair; cattle (four fairs a year) and sheep (three fairs a year) in the market place. As the number of fairs increased in the nineteenth century, so did the complaints about the mess, the smell and the runaways. In 1858 the cattle and sheep fairs moved to Treasurers Garth (off Blossomgate), but within three years they were back in the market square. Cattle, sheep and swine moved to North Street in 1881. In 1892 there were auction marts in the Brewster Terrace area as well as at the North Road site, previously a brickworks. Two years later, weekly livestock sales were again being held in the market square. Responding to growing complaints, the Board of Agriculture banned the sale of sheep, cattle and swine in 1898, but withdrew the order a few months later when the north side of the market place was concreted. In 1903 cattle were restricted to the southern corner of the square, where the cobbles had been concreted over three years earlier, but older Riponians remember cattle sales at the north end after that. The council suggested a change of site for the cattle market in 1912, but the Agricultural Association's protests won the day - the cattle stayed and a water trough was provided.[46] The North Road auction mart closed following the outbreak of foot and mouth disease in 2001/2 and did not reopen.

It was in the market place that the people congregated. For royal proclamations, the mayor and corporation walked three times round the cross. A bonfire would be lit for a celebration, and ale and wine would flow at the corporation's expense. It is still the principal civic focal point and the city's busiest thoroughfare. In the 1930s the puppeteer Walter Wilkinson described the scene when he arrived in Ripon:

'From the Cathedral I got into the market, the most genuine country market I have seen for years. Farmers' wives and daughters were standing about with baskets of fresh eggs and new-made butter; sober men, who looked like the growers themselves, were weighing out the vegetables; there were flowers and fruits, and animals in the folds, and at one corner the tweeded farmers, real men with beards, stood conversing in groups ... The customers and stall holders were all old friends ... It all seemed more like a festival than an ordinary weekly shopping.' [47]

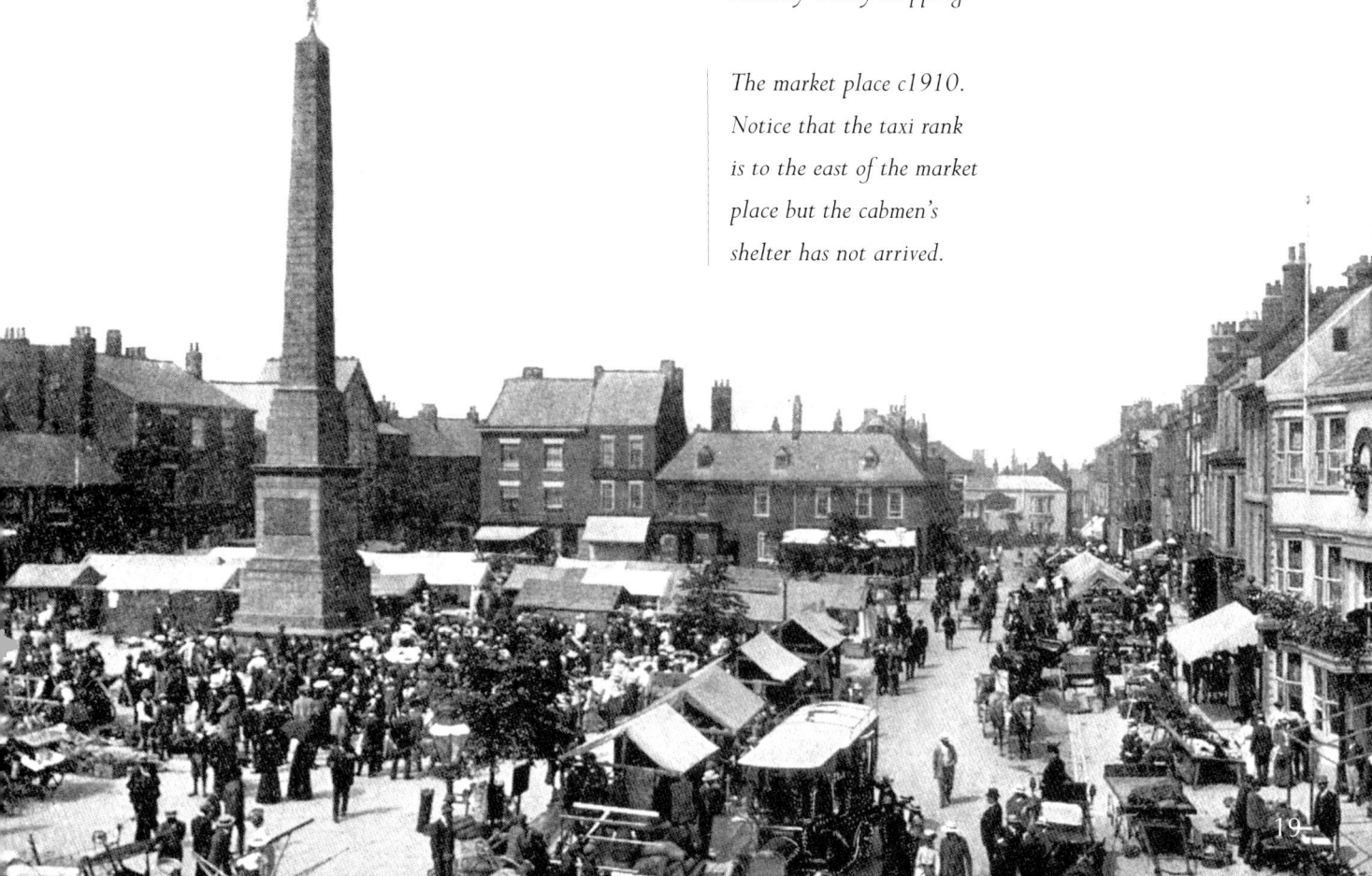

The market place c1910. Notice that the taxi rank is to the east of the market place but the cabmen's shelter has not arrived.

Monastery, Minster, Cathedral

This picture, by the late Canon Ashworth, attempted to interpret Eddius's description of Wilfrid's church at Ripon, but from recent archaeological evidence is now thought to be unreliable.

Ripon enters the record books about AD 657 when a grant of thirty, or as Bede says forty, hides of land[48] was given to Abbot Eata of Melrose for a new monastery, by Alchfrid, prince of Northumbria. In Ripon parish at the time of Domesday, a hide, or carucate, varied from 48 acres (19ha) in Studley to 128 acres (48ha) in Hewick, enough to support a family according to the quality of the land.[49]

Celtic monks lived austere lives. Their monastery would have been a circle of small, beehive-shaped, timber and turf huts around a wooden church. No traces survive on the traditional site between Priest Lane and St. Marysgate - roughly where Ripon House now stands and probably running down to the river. The guest master was the young St. Cuthbert. Bede tells of how, after attending to one particular guest at Ripon, Cuthbert 'understood that he had entertained an angel'[50].

Three centuries later, Cuthbert again rested at Ripon, carried in his coffin by monks fleeing from Danish attacks on Lindisfarne. Eata's monks did not stay long at Ripon. Disagreement between the Celtic and Roman churches, superficially about the dating of Easter, but crucially over the validity of the Celtic priesthood, came to a head at that time.[51]

Wilfrid had been born in AD 634 to a noble Northumbrian Anglian family. At fourteen he was accepted into the royal court at Bamburgh, becoming friendly with Prince Alchfrid. He studied under the queen's chaplain, and became increasingly conscious of the differences between the Latin and Celtic rites. Wilfrid was sent to attend a paralysed nobleman retiring to the monastery at Lindisfarne. A gifted student, he spent four years there, after which he was granted permission to visit Rome, where he was captivated by the liturgy and splendour of the Latin Church. Having made his monastic vows at Lyons, he returned to York in 658. There are two interpretations of what happened at Ripon in 660: in one, Abbot Eata declined to adopt the Latin (Benedictine) rites and withdrew: in the other he was evicted. For Ripon the result was the same: Eata and the Celtic monks were out, and in 661 Wilfrid took possession of the monastery at Ripon.

The difficulties for the Court, with both rites in operation, had to be resolved.[52] In 664 the synod of Whitby was called by the king, where Wilfrid presented the case for Rome so eloquently that his arguments won the day. Subsequently he was appointed bishop of the vast diocese of Northumbria, in addition to his posts as abbot of Ripon and Hexham. Wilfrid's appointment as bishop with his seat at York

Ripon Cathedral crypt. One of the only two sites in England where it is possible to stand completely enclosed within walls and roofs built during the first century of English Christianity.

starts the path to the claims, after the Conquest, by the Norman archbishops of York to the liberty (or franchise) of Ripon. Wilfrid himself was never titled Archbishop of York, a post not created until after his death.[53] 'Liberty' was a term loosely applied to many manors of little significance, but the manor of Ripon, if not in size, was high in the scale of franchises and became almost a county in itself, the rule of the archbishop taking over from that of the king.

Wilfrid's visits to Europe inspired building in the grand manner. The stone abbey churches at Ripon and Hexham were described as the finest buildings west of the Alps. Their crypts survive: both contain re-used Roman stones.[54]

At Ripon, Wilfrid chose a new site for his monastery: *'In Ripon he [Wilfrid] built and completed from the foundations in the earth up to the roof a church of dressed stone; supported by various columns and side aisles to a great height with many windows, arched vaults and winding cloister'.*[55]

Monastery, Minster, Cathedral

The 1997 excavations by the York Archaeological Trust revealed not only the evidence of floor surfaces pointing to the seventh-century church and of re-used Roman blocks in the passage roofs, but also of a technique thought to be unique in Anglo-Saxon England: the construction of the vault of the main chamber used truncated wedge-shaped stones, between stone ribs, fixed in position to the top of the ribs by a thick layer of pink mortar, typical of the kind used for the walls of the crypt chamber noted in earlier excavations. The space above was infilled with sand to create a level floor to the church above. Archaeologist Dr Richard Hall raised the question of where Wilfrid learnt this technique.[56]

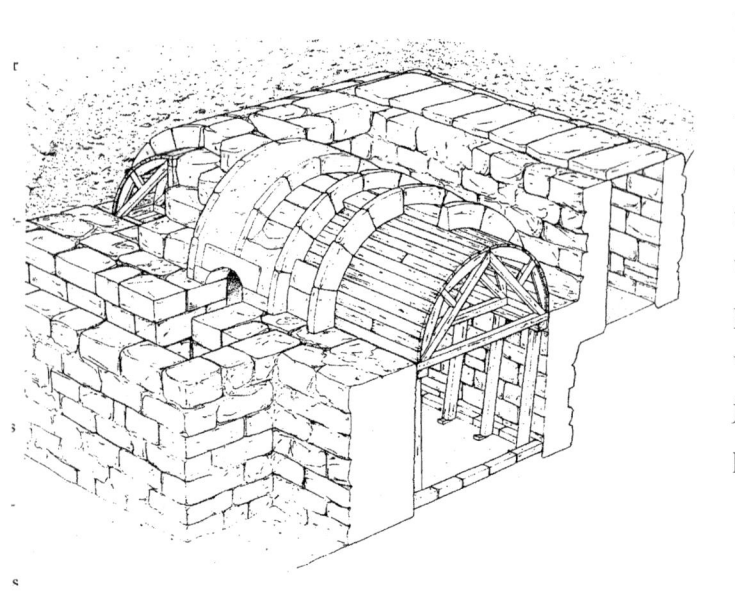

Wilfrid imported European craftsmen not only to build but also to adorn his churches. To Ripon he gave an illuminated copy of the Gospels written in gold on purple parchment, housed in a gold case set with precious gems. It was lost, most likely in the mid-tenth century, when English monasteries were being destroyed and their manuscripts plundered.[57]

Wilfrid was controversial, autocratic and volatile, He is usually presented as an example of how not to succeed in the political and ecclesiastical world of the seventh century.[58] But he has his defenders, who argue that he has been unfairly vilified over the centuries. He was a great missionary and acquirer of land to endow his monasteries. Under Germanic law, monasteries were presumed to belong to their founders: abbots like Wilfrid operated within this framework.

He offended many powerful people by what were seen as high handed attitudes, for example, rejecting Celtic bishops for his ordination to the priesthood and waiting until the French bishop of Wessex, Agilbert, was available. For his consecration as bishop, Prince Alchfrid agreed to pay the enormous costs for Wilfrid and a retinue of 120 to go to Compiègne, where twelve Catholic bishops officiated at his consecration in 665. Upon his return, Wilfrid found that not only had he been deposed as bishop but also that Prince Alchfrid had disappeared. The reasons are perhaps lost in the mists of time, but Alchfrid's father was not impressed by the vast expenditure on Wilfrid's journey, the length of his absence and rumours of plots by the prince against his father.

Artist's impression of how St. Wilfrid's crypt was built.

Wilfrid was re-instated in 669, and the next decade saw the building of his abbey churches at Ripon and Hexham, and the restoration of his Cathedral at York, but in 678 he was banished. He set off again to Rome, returning two years later vindicated by papal decree, but he was imprisoned and then exiled. In 686 he returned to Northumbria for five years until he was once again banished, spending the next ten years in Mercia and Kent where he met Eddius, who became his chaplain and biographer, and returned with him to teach Benedictine chanting to the Ripon monks.

In 702 a council was called at Austerfield to settle Wilfrid's claims. The case went against him and he was dispossessed. Once more he went to Rome, returning in 704-5 with another papal decree. Another council was called, this time at the River Nidd. With some reluctance a compromise was agreed for Wilfrid's return: to fill the vacancy caused by the death of Bosa as bishop of York, John of Beverley would transfer from Hexham to York, and Wilfrid would replace John as bishop of Hexham.

By this time Wilfrid was an old man and, whilst he must have hoped for more, at least he could continue to exercise episcopal office and he had regained control of Ripon and Hexham. At Hexham, close to his great abbey church of St. Andrew, he built another, dedicated to St. Mary, in thanksgiving for a miraculous restoration to health whilst he was returning from Rome in 705. Some thirty miles (45km) north-east of Paris he had become desperately ill and, unconscious, he was carried on a litter to the town of Meaux.

After five days, the archangel Michael appeared to him telling him that, through the intercession of the Virgin Mary, his life had been spared for four years, during which time he should build a church in Mary honour. In failing health he did as the archangel had instructed, divided out his wealth and appointed his successors.

An Anglo Saxon Bishop

Monastery, Minster, Cathedral

Wilfrid died at Oundle in 709-10. When one adds up the time he spent in Ripon, it is relatively short, but in fulfilment of his wishes, his body was carried to Ripon for burial on the south side of his church.[59] Recent excavations have sought to trace the site and, whilst a grave was found, the remains were of a fifteenth-century female.

According to the Life of St. Oswald, some time between 972 and 992 Wilfrid's remains were moved to the north side of the church by Archbishop Oswald of Canterbury.[60] There is some disagreement about this incident because, in the twelfth century, Eadmer recorded Wilfrid's remains as having been transferred to Canterbury by Odo, archbishop from 941-58,[61] but the earlier 'Life of St. Oswald' account is at least as good and arguably the more reliable of the two. Possibly seeking to justify the enshrining of St. Wilfrid's remains at Ripon in the thirteenth century, efforts to reconcile the two accounts have claimed Canterbury's relics to be Wilfrid II.[62]

Wilfrid was a man of international vision whose actions prevented the isolation of England at that time, and no one greater has been as closely associated with Ripon, but Wilfrid was never titled 'bishop of Ripon'. With other titles and at various times he was abbot of Ripon, abbot of Hexham, bishop of Northumbria and bishop of York. In 681 the archbishop of Canterbury created a new diocese, and Eadhead became the first bishop of Ripon with his seat in the abbey church. He did not last long and no one succeeded him. As one of a small group of privileged churches (matrices ecclesiae) within the archdiocese of York, in the later medieval period Ripon Minster was sometimes styled 'Cathedral', but it was not until

Fourteenth century alabaster, possibly from an altar at Ripon and thought to represent St. Wilfrid from what may be the 'St. Wilfrid Burning Iron' on his right arm.

1836, with the establishment of the new diocese of Ripon, that Ripon Minster became a Cathedral in its own right, the first new diocese to be formed after the Reformation.

The Danish invasions are generally said to have brought much destruction to the country and it was thought that Wilfrid's church was destroyed in AD 860, but there is no evidence for this. Around 886, as leader and spokesman 'of all councillors of the English race', King Alfred made a treaty with the Danish King Guthrum of East Anglia, which left the Danes with control north of Watling Street (roughly London to Chester) - the Danelaw, of which Ripon was very much a part. The treaty seems to have allowed that 'Englishmen, under their rule, would have the same wergeld [monetary value] as Danes of their own class, and as Englishmen in Wessex'. How far this applied outside East Anglia is uncertain, but Northumbria's relationships with the kings of Wessex began to develop from Alfred's time.[63] It may be this treaty that gave rise to the story of the King Alfred charter at Ripon, but the claim of Alfred granting a charter specifically to Ripon in 886 is not credible. It was not until Alfred's successor, Edward the Elder, had over-run Mercia and East Anglia that he received the Danes' submission.

Trouble arose again in 924 with the succession of Athelstan, Alfred's grandson. Campaigning to restore Anglo-Saxon control, Athelstan conquered the Northumbrians in 926. His second campaign culminated in the Battle of Brunnanburh in 937, in which he led an alliance of West Saxons and Mercians against Constantine, king of Scotland. The site of the battle is much disputed, recently claimed as being in the Wirral, but Athelstan is said to have vowed that if he were successful in the battle he would grant privileges to the churches at Beverley, Ripon and York. As a result, it was claimed, the liberty of St. Wilfrid was created at Ripon and a chartered sanctuary established, one league around the church, marked by eight boundary crosses.

Before the Norman Conquest, it is almost impossible to separate Church and State, with spiritual and secular laws being administered together. It was only later that the Anglo-Saxon laws were written down in the Latin alphabet by the clerical scribes.[64] When, in the thirteenth century, the Crown began the Quo Warranto hearings demanding proof to the title of franchises, it is not easy to understand why the Athelstan charters were put forward as the foundation of the archbishop's title, as their benefits were to the church at Ripon, the only reference to the archbishop being a restriction of his rights.[65] In 1228 the 'Athelstan charter' was presented to the king's justices by the Ripon canons to support their claim to ancient rights against the claims of the archbishop. Such 'pious forgeries' were not uncommon at the time; and it was accepted by the jury. Such a grant could well have been made by Athelstan, but probably with fewer privileges than claimed in 1228.[66] Further Quo Warranto proceedings followed in 1279-80 and again in 1292, the record of which gives full particulars of the liberty privileges. However, in 1419 it was confirmed that 'the king's justices were not to have their cognizance within the liberty and that neither the king's treasurer nor the barons of the exchequer should take any process against the archbishop's justices for estreats [fines/ forfeitures] of their sessions'. Free warren and chase (hunting rights) in his demesne lands - that part of the manor kept for his own use-were also granted to the archbishop, under a penalty to trespassers of £100.[67]

Monastery, Minster, Cathedral

Amongst the early rights claimed was that of sanctuary. All parish churches could grant sanctuary for periods varying between three and seven days, but at a chartered sanctuary a refugee could shelter within the churchyard for some thirty days and nights whilst the clergy tried to bring peace. If he chose to 'abjure the realm', the fugitive was escorted to the coroner, usually at the sanctuary boundary, and could decide to face trial or be deported. In chartered sanctuary towns like Ripon there was another option: to become a grithman (or frithman), a sworn servant of the Church, surrendering his possessions, but allowed to follow his craft or trade providing he remained within the sanctuary bounds.

At Beverley, sanctuary began a league (about one and a third miles/2km) from the church, with a second boundary at the town edge, a third at the churchyard, others at the church door, the choir and finally the sanctuary seat itself. As the refugee crossed the different bounds, increasingly severe penalties faced the vengeance seeker who molested him.[68] The charters of Beverley and Ripon are so closely linked that it is likely a similar system applied at both, and that the ring of eight sanctuary crosses at Ripon was sited where the liberty/township boundary crossed the eight roads radiating from the town.[69] If this argument is accepted, depending on topographical features and how strictly a league was measured, Sharow and Kangel (Archangel) Crosses may have been part of an inner, rather than an outer, ring.

In AD 948, about a decade after Athelstan's death, according to the Anglo-Saxon Chronicles, Athelstan's half-brother, Eadred, king of the English, *'ravaged all Northumbria because they had taken Eric for their king. In that ravaging the Minster at Ripon was burnt down, that St.Wilferth had built.'* [70]

In the more settled times which followed across the country, until the reforms of Dunstan, monks were displaced by laymen and clerks.[71] By 995 the church at Ripon was able to house the remains of St. Cuthbert for some three months, suggesting that the buildings must have recovered sufficiently by then. This is one of the obscure times in the history of the Minster, and it is not clear when it ceased to be a monastery and was reconstituted as a chapter of secular canons (a group of clergy serving a Cathedral or collegiate church),[72] but prebends - the estates which provided the income for the canons - were founded by the 1060s at York, Beverley and Ripon. If these were for priests, as seems likely, it would be the beginning of Ripon's second ecclesiastical foundation - as a collegiate church. The Domesday survey also refers to canons at Ripon.

In the aftermath of the Norman Conquest, Ripon was to be rocked again with the 'Harrying of the North' in 1069, the devastation wreaked by the Conqueror for the continued resistance in the North of England. The Domesday survey recorded, in the manor eight villeins (villagers), ten bordars (husbandmen), six ploughs, a mill and a fishery, the taxable value of the archbishop's manor having fallen from £32 to £7 10s.

The earliest part of the church at Ripon, apart from the Saxon crypt, was thought to be the so-called Norman crypt, undercroft, or 'bone house', presently the Chapel of the Resurrection, sometimes dated to around 1080. However, this structure is now regarded as no earlier than Archbishop Roger's church of c1175, and it is thought that the late Saxon church could well have survived, with some re-building by Archbishop Thomas (1070-1100), until Roger built his 'new basilica', of which the chapter house block or 'south annexe' formed part.

Bones from earlier burials were stored in the undercroft of the chapter house (Norman crypt) till 1865 when they were interred in a large pit in the newly-extended graveyard.

Monastery, Minster, Cathedral

Having no original external access, the undercroft may have started life as a treasury, accessed by steps inside the wall dividing the chapter house from the south transept. The slightly later chapter house rests above.[73] Close to the entrances to the town, three medieval hospital chapels, St. Mary Magdalen's, St. John's and St. Anne's, all sited at the river crossings, offered 'hospitality' to travellers, the poor and the sick, fulfilling the Church's 'Seven Works of Mercy'. Chantry chapels were later founded within two of them.

Across the country, neglect, declining revenues or changes of use meant that many medieval hospital foundations had disappeared well before the Reformation, but the majority of those still active in 1547 survived the dissolution of the chantries either by local corporations buying or begging them from the Crown, or by their being subsequently revived.[74] The archbishops of York controlled the Ripon hospitals and appointed masters until 1544, when Archbishop Holgate surrendered his rights to Henry VIII, but Mary Tudor restored them to Archbishop Heath ten years later.[75] From 1688, with one exception, the deans of Ripon have been masters of both St. Mary's and St. John's.

St. Anne's, standing by the old Archer Bridge, was the smallest, and is the only hospital chapel whose complete medieval structure can still be visualised. According to tradition it was founded by one of the Nevilles, dukes of Northumberland, for *'eight poor folks, men and women, the which in time past have been of honest behaviour, now in age and poverty continuing their life in prayer and devotion for their helpers and benefactors, having none other worldly goods to their sustentation but relief and alms of Christian people'*. There is a reference to Annusgate as early as 1228; and Agnesgate occurs in 1462. The earliest documentary evidence for St. Anne's dates from 1438, but parts of the remains are of an earlier style. It was formerly called the Massendew or 'Maidens Due', a corruption of Maison de Dieu - house of God. The small chapel at the eastern end of the building was joined to a 'nave' divided into two dormitories, each with four beds plus two common beds *'for every true travelling man or woman that hath noe spending and there he may be eased one day and night in fulfilling of the seven workes of mercy'*. There was accommodation for a chaplain at the west end of the building. After the Reformation, St. Anne's Hospital sheltered eight poor widows, and its masters became the mayor and corporation.

Internal arrangement at St. Anne's Hospital.

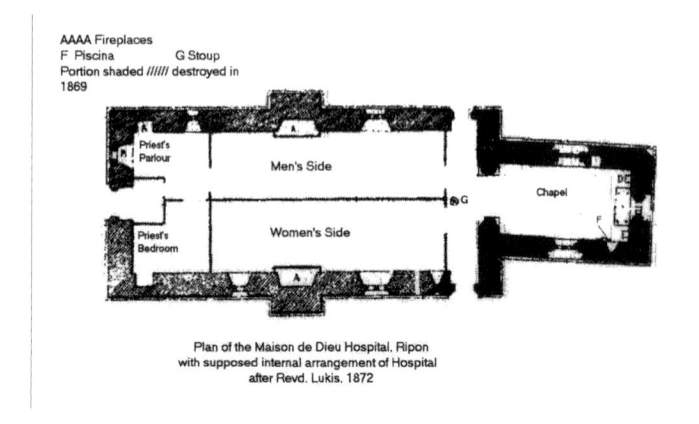

Plan of the Maison de Dieu Hospital, Ripon with supposed internal arrangement of Hospital after Revd. Lukis. 1872

Because it was not wealthily endowed, St. Anne's did not suffer the depredations of pluralist clerics and continued to carry out good works over the years with meagre resources, particularly supported in later years by the Greenwood family of West Lodge, whose gifts paid for the almshouses built in 1869. Ripon Civic Society put the chapel ruins into a sound state of repair in the early 1970s. During the 1980s the accommodation was upgraded for four women residents.

The ruins of St. Anne's Hospital Chapel.

Monastery, Minster, Cathedral

The earliest of the chapels is St. John's, at the crossing of the Skell from Bondgate. It was founded by Thomas II, archbishop of York from 1109 to 1114. He gave land when Ripon was 'in a wild state' to provide hospitality for poor travellers and, after the area was cleared, 'to support poor clerks keeping their schools at Ripon, four or five of whom were to have soup twice a week'. David de Wollore, master of the rolls and canon of Ripon, appointed master in 1340, provided new equipment and endowments for a chaplain and poor boys attending the grammar schools in Ripon, but before long much was again misappropriated and new endowments became rare. Like its sister hospitals,

St. John's Medieval chapel towards the end of its life, after the National School had moved to Priest Lane.

The chapel of St. Mary Magdalen stands as a reminder of the twelfth century hospital which it originally served.

St. John's survived as almshouses. Its mastership formed part of clergy income from 1604, responsibility passing from the archbishop to the dean. In the early nineteenth century St. John's was supporting only two women, who were receiving £1 7s 6d a year and being cared for in an apartment in Bondgate. A chaplain was paid £1 a year. By the early eighteenth century the chapel was in use as a school and had not been used regularly as a place of worship for many years although, perhaps 'at the pleasure of the master or chaplain', a service was held on St. John the Baptist's Day until 1722-3. In 1812 it was converted into a National school,[76] and in 1818 there were 210 boys on the roll. Commissioners were appointed to investigate irregularities in the finances, and forty years of legal wrangling ended in 1866 in the Court of Chancery. In 1868 a new chapel of ease was built, followed ten years later by six almshouses.

The hospital of St. Mary Magdalen, sometimes called the Maudlins, is perhaps best known as the Leper Chapel. It was founded by archbishop Thurstan of York (archbishop from 1114-39) for a chaplain and secular brothers and sisters to minister to lepers and blind priests born within the liberty of Ripon. Riponshire lepers were to be given: a coat (called a 'rak' or 'bak') and two pairs of shoes a year: a loaf and

Monastery, Minster, Cathedral

half a pitcher of beer daily: on flesh days a portion of flesh, and three herrings on maigre-days, ie meagre or short-ration days.[77] The hospital was set up not long after the first Crusade and 'leprosy' was probably an umbrella term for a variety of skin diseases. Lepers from outside the liberty could obtain a night's food and lodging, as could any other stranger, or travelling cleric.

By the early fourteenth century there were neither lepers nor sisters at St. Mary's Hospital, but the poor could claim a dole of food on the 22nd July, St. Mary Magdalen's day. The foundation changed sometime after 1241 to a master, not necessarily a priest, and a chaplain. There may have been as many as six chantry priests attached to this small chapel in the early fourteenth century, when the leper house was demolished. After the dissolution of the monasteries, Marmaduke Bradley, last abbot of Fountains, spent the rest of his life as master, although it is uncertain if he lived there.

In 1674, under Dean Hooke's mastership, the almshouses at St. Mary's were rebuilt to provide accommodation for six poor widows. A partial fall of the roof is recorded in 1856,[78] which may have been influential in the provision of a new chapel in 1868, now redundant, built at the expense of George Mason of Copt Hewick. In 1875 the almshouses near the Victorian chapel were rebuilt as part of a land deal with the marquess of Ripon; the six to the south of the medieval chapel were added in 1890. June 1897 brought the restoration of the medieval chapel, including the *'surrounding objectionable buildings cleared away, walls strengthened by buttresses and ancient tiles re-laid'*.[79] March 1917 saw the old chapel of St. Mary's again being restored. Rubble and brickwork blocking the windows were removed. Hen runs and pigsties adjacent were demolished. The work included underpinning the foundations and inserting new purlins (timbers) in the roof. Some of the plaster was stripped from the internal walls, to reveal a scroll fresco at the northeastern end of the building and an early sculptured piece of red sandstone on the south wall. Work to restore the lead flashing to the roof and the brick floor was undertaken, and the plain diamond paned windows were re-glazed, retaining the original glass where possible. The fifteenth-century, late Perpendicular wooden screen recovered from the Cathedral was re-erected, heavily restored.

Services continued in the nineteenth-century chapel at St. Mary's until it was taken out of use following a further restoration of the medieval chapel in the 1980s, supervised by Mr Sebastian Rowe of Ripon. During an associated archaeological dig, bodies were discovered to the north. Burials at a chapel are unusual. Normally they would have been reserved to the parish church, but this chapel was licensed for burials in 1341, by which time the leper house had been demolished.

Nothing remains of the medieval structure of St. Mary's apart from the 'leper' chapel itself. The gritstone fabric of the western section of the building is thought to be original; the limestone, eastern, later. Over the south door is a Norman arch with a later, Early English, arch inserted. In the north wall is a low-side (so-called leper) window, although the 1854 plan shows a low-side window at the south-west, the usual position for such a window. In the sanctuary stands a pre-Reformation stone altar, in front of which is a thirteenth century tessellated pavement with a circular medallion, said to be Roman.

Between 1154 and 1181, when Roger pont l'Eveque was archbishop of York, the Minster - the building which we recognise today as Ripon Cathedral - began to take shape. Architectural interpretation dates its beginnings to about 1175. Because of Roger's complicity in the murder, in 1170, of his arch-enemy Thomas á Becket, it is often put forward that the Ripon work followed as an act of expiation. The opposite has also been suggested: that it could have been Roger's way of countering the Becket cult, rapidly emerging at Canterbury, by elevating Wilfrid, a readily available saint without a shrine in the North, at an early religious site. It has recently been argued that Roger had been funding the ongoing work and his grant of £1,000 was made as death approached, but that it never reached the chapter, being *'confiscated with the rest of Roger's treasury by Henry II'*. Certainly the death of its patron in 1184 brought a scaling down of the original concept for high stone vaults over the choir and transepts, in favour of timber roofs.

How much Roger's successor, Geoffrey Plantagenet, illegitimate son of Henry II, contributed to the completion of the Minster now comes into question. Having been deprived of his position by the pope and of his revenues by King Richard, Geoffrey was left with only the manor of Ripon, where he lived until he visited Rome and was re-instated

Ripon Minster west front prior to the removal of the western spires in 1664. Care should be taken interpreting artistic licence in this well-known drawing by Daniel King.

Monastery, Minster, Cathedral

as archbishop by the pope, and in gratitude, (Stuart Harrison and Paul Barker propose), it may be Geoffrey who was persuaded to complete the Minster church at Ripon. He was certainly involved with the church. Peter of Blois, highly esteemed canon of Ripon, invited Geoffrey to write and dedicate a life of St. Wilfrid to him.

Parts of the twelfth-century building can still be seen: in the walls just inside the west door, the round arches in the central tower, and the transepts.[80] In 1224, Archbishop Walter de Gray moved St. Wilfrid's remains, which he is said to have found complete, to a new shrine, displaying the head separately and encouraging pilgrims by giving indulgences (the remission of a specified number of years in purgatory) to all who visited it. He was also responsible for the very fine west front (originally crowned with spires) and added, if it was not there already, a spire to the central tower. A hundred years later, when the townspeople took refuge in the Minster against the invading Scots, battlements were added to the transepts and possibly then the protective wall built below the east window, since removed.[81]

Ripon Minster about 1818 showing the wall thought to have been added in the early fourteenth century as protection against the Scots. Later, as graves were cleared for new occupants or for the addition of the nave aisles, remains were placed in the space behind the wall. They were reburied when the wall was removed and the graveyard extended from the 1830s.

Top: A view through the sixteenth century arches towards the twelfth century Norman transitional structure remaining inside the Cathedral.

Above: Looking east down the Cathedral nave towards the choir, the rounded 12th century arch and its supporting columns on the left contrast with the later 16th century work around it.

Various estates, called prebends, had been established to provide income for the canons. After 1301 they took the name of their principal hamlet. In addition to Stanwick near Richmond - often the wealthiest, whose holder was required to be resident and acted more like a dean - there were Nunwick, (Little)Thorpe, Studley, Givendale, Monkton (the resident canon treasurer) and Skelton. The holders were to provide and maintain houses for themselves in Ripon for their periods of residence, but many merely drew the income and rarely came to Ripon, paying less well-educated vicars to perform their duties.

As a result, the houses became neglected: Thorpe Prebend House, for example, was used as a bell

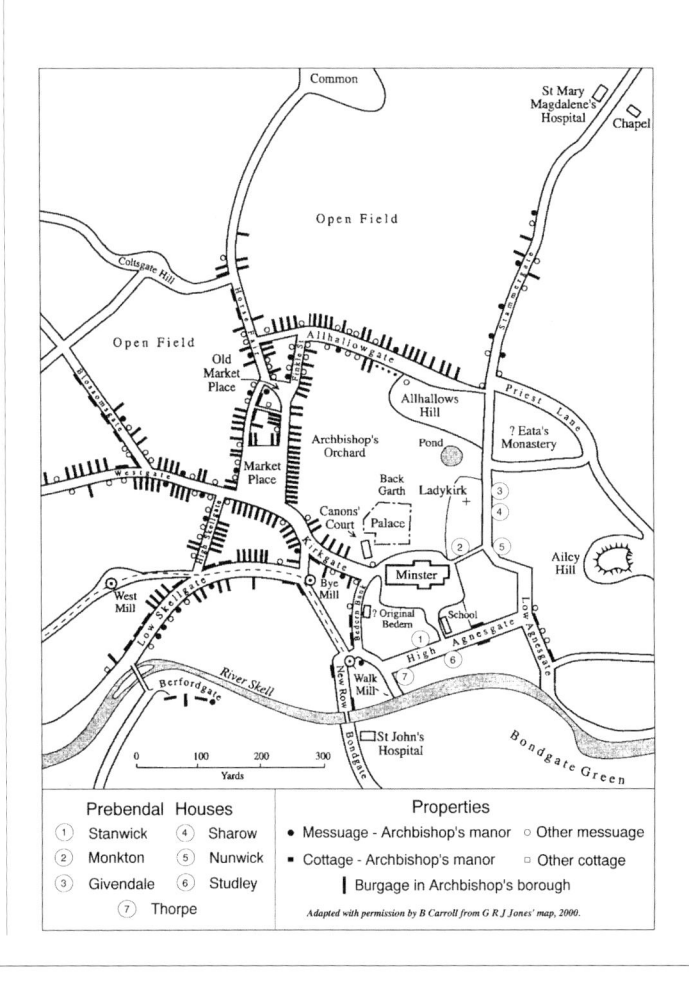

Prebendal Houses		Properties
① Stanwick ④ Sharow		• Messuage - Archbishop's manor ○ Other messuage
② Monkton ⑤ Nunwick		■ Cottage - Archbishop's manor □ Other cottage
③ Givendale ⑥ Studley		❘ Burgage in Archbishop's borough
⑦ Thorpe		*Adapted with permission by B Carroll from G R J Jones' map, 2000.*

35

Monastery, Minster, Cathedral

foundry in the fourteenth century; others became quarries. As a 'peculiar' - sometimes also spelt 'peculier' - the parish of Ripon was outside the authority of the normal hierarchy of the Church, in Ripon's case of the archdeacon of Richmond. The parish was controlled by the Minster chapter, with the rural dean of Ripon sitting as 'Dean of Christianity' at the 'Court Christian', where parishioners would plead against charges of defamation, immorality, neglect of religious duties and so on. Under the protection of the Athelstan charter, defendants used the system of compurgation - calling witnesses to join their oaths to the accused - to prove themselves innocent. Penalties for those found guilty included beatings, walking barefoot in the processions, being suspended from entering the church, or excommunication.

This building served as the courthouse for the medieval canons, (the canon fee court) then as the jail for the liberty of Ripon and in the 19thC as a debtors prison.

A record of 1340 preserves the duties of the chapter's bailiff: *'Robert de Sawley came into the chapter house at Ripon and claimed to hold his toft and two bovates of land and pasture in Bondgate by the service of bearing a rod at the chapter court and in processions at the greater festivals, paying a rent of 18d. It was found on examination of records that his duties were also to summon the court of free tenants, levy amercements (fines, punishments), make attachments (arrests), go on every Wednesday and Friday with the tasters to present defaulters of bread and ale and to levy tolls on all sales and purchases in the Canon Fee'.*[82]

Ripon and its surrounding area was a liberty, which meant it was also outside the authority of the sheriff. The liberty covered an area similar to the peculiar and comprised two secular jurisdictions, one belonging to the archbishop as lord of the manor, and the other, known as the liberty of St. Wilfrid, to the chapter of the Minster.[83] The archbishop maintained that his rights were pre-eminent. During the early thirteenth century the power struggle culminated in an important court case, reference to which has already been made. The Minster chapter complained that the archbishop's bailiff and the sheriff of Yorkshire had, by force, invaded the rights of the church at Ripon.

The sheriff and the bailiff argued that the chapter had no rights to what they claimed. The chapter had already successfully defended its rights, and in 1228 produced what we now know to be the 'pious forgery' of a charter from King Athelstan. Despite the archbishop himself giving evidence, judgement was awarded in favour of the canons.

The west front of Ripon Cathedral.

Monastery, Minster, Cathedral

Discovered during an archaeological investigation in 1977 to the north of the Cathedral this ornament, of twisted gold thread inlaid with amber and garnets, has been dated to the last quarter of the seventh century - the time of Saint Wilfrid - and may have formed part of a prelate's cross.

About this time the archbishop built a palace near York, after which archbishops of York, whilst continuing to enjoy the hunting and fishing of their Ripon park, shifted their principal residence to York. It is said that Archbishop de Gray was only resident at Ripon eight times in his forty years as archbishop, preferring Knaresborough instead, suggesting that the Ripon palace was insufficiently secure, or had been allowed to deteriorate. Part of the Minster choir was rebuilt in the 1290s, with the great east window very shortly afterwards. In 1310 the bishop of Galloway, who had been consecrated at Ripon, had to return to re-consecrate the graveyard after two women fought so severely that blood was shed. A similar desecration occurred in 1469.

Besides the Minster, there was another, possibly earlier, parish church in Ripon, Allhallows. It is thought to have stood on the mound towards the bottom of Allhallowgate.[84] There was also a chapel, the 'Ladykirk', on St. Marysgate; the three chapels associated with the hospitals of St. Anne, St. Mary Magdalen and St. John; and chapels at North Bridge, Hewick Bridge and Bishopton Bridge.

In the medieval period, most of those who worked with their heads rather than their hands were part of the Church; would have been admitted to one of its clerical orders; and could claim its protection and be tried by its courts, avoiding the barbaric punishments meted out by the king's courts.

After being found guilty in the bishop's court, the cleric could be sentenced to be degraded.

Records survive of clerics found guilty of burglary, horse stealing, theft and murder, who were brought before the archbishop at Ripon. After acknowledging their guilt, the archbishop pronounced sentence. They then moved outside the Minster and at the west door they were stripped of their clerical robes, whilst the archbishop dismissed them with the awesome words: *'By the authority of God the Omnipotent, Father, Son and Holy Ghost, and by our authority, we take from you the clerical habit, we put you away, we degrade you, we deprive you and strip you of whatever rank, benefice, or clerical privilege you possess.'* [85] In the papal records of 1403, a letter of Pope Boniface IX survives, threatening excommunication for those who robbed the church at Ripon of its muniments and its pewter, and its gold and silver treasures.[86] It was in many ways a bad time for the Church. Vicars, proctors (court officials/ agents) and sometimes even laymen would be given short-term contracts and paid a paltry sum to undertake the duties. Archbishop Corbridge ordered that the prebendal houses be put in order and ruled against farming out the prebends without his authority. In 1303 he laid down that not only should the vicars be permanently appointed and paid six marks (£4) a year, but that they should provide themselves with a bedern (prayer house) near the Minster to live communally. As a result, Le Walk Milne Bank became Bedern Bank.[87] In 1415, the archbishop re-organised the chaplains and gave land for a new bedern - the site of the Old Deanery - and paid most of the cost of building, but by 1515 that bedern was in disrepair.

Standing on the site of the fifteenth century bedern, the Old Deanery dates from the early years of the seventeenth century. It was for use by the canon in residence under the 1604 foundation, but in practice was occupied by the dean.

Monastery, Minster, Cathedral

With high levels of absenteeism amongst the medieval canons, it is hardly surprising that the Minster fell into a poor state of repair. Even so, in the fourteenth century the Lady Chapel was built, unusually, above the chapter house. Part of the Lady Loft, as it was called, was used for storing books from the fifteenth century and became the library in the seventeenth century.

The central spire was rebuilt in 1396, but about 1450 the tower collapsed, causing much damage. Reconstruction of the nave began with the south aisle in 1502-3, but was never finished. Each canon agreed to pay six marks (£4) a year for five years to the fabric fund, except the prebendary of Stanwick who was only required to pay four marks. Half of the common fund was to go to the fabric. By 1506 work had almost stopped, partly for lack of funds and partly because workmen would not come into the town for fear of the plague. In 1513 the foundations of the north aisle were laid. Plague and pestilence continued on and off from 1485 to 1636. Country people had their children baptised on the common pasture rather than come into the town. In three months during 1558, fifty-nine Stonebridgegate residents died *'of a strange ague'*.

From 1489-94 the Ripon woodcarvers were largely responsible for the very fine set of choir stalls. The medieval carvers appear to have had some freedom in the choice of decoration, especially of the undersides of the ledges of these tip-up misericord seats. Ripon has more religious and moral subjects than most but even so, hidden away out of sight of the clergy, in a canopy of the choir stalls, a man exposing himself must have escaped the attentions of Cromwellian and subsequent destructions.

William Bromflet was the carver named in the C16th contracts, and it was he who travelled to York and Hull arranging supplies. He was paid 6d (2½p) a day, as was Christopher Bromflet.

The 'Jonah' misericords in the Cathedral choir stall.

Three other men, Ranulf Bromflet, Robert Dowyff and Radulf Turrett, were paid 4d (1½ p) a day, and doubtless assistants and labourers would be involved as well. To complete the work in such a short space of time required skilful organisation.

A clear regional style can be identified, although 'Ripon School' is thought by some experts to be overly specific. The Ripon carvers' work is regarded as amongst the best in the North. No two misericords are the same.[88] A key emblem in the carving at Ripon is the pomegranate, a popular resurrection symbol which fell out of use in England in the twelfth century, but is thought to have been reintroduced around 1500 following the link between the English monarchy and the French house of Aragon, in whose coat of arms it appeared. If this were the case, together with one at Windsor of 1480, Ripon's would be an early example of its re-use in this country. The fruit is usually shown with split skin and the seeds showing through.

A new canopy for the bishop's stall was provided in 1812, but this was subsequently moved to the consistory court.[89] The work of adding aisles and rebuilding the nave was almost complete by 1538. The master mason responsible for the work, Christopher Scune, was not a local man. The Perpendicular architecture, developed in England during the fourteenth and fifteenth centuries, and characterised by the vertical lines of the tracery, must place the nave amongst the finest as well as the latest of the style.

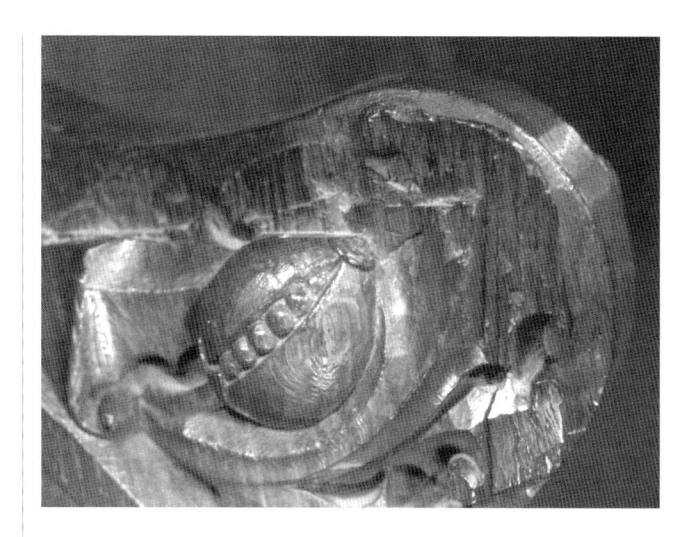

Although this Cathedral bench-end has been damaged the pomegranate has survived relatively unscathed.

Monastery, Minster, Cathedral

Cathedral Choir looking East showing the box pews which filled it after the fall of the spire for some two hundred years.

The attack on relics in 1538 is the likely date for the destruction of St. Wilfrid's shrine. The following year saw the suppression of Fountains Abbey and the return of Marmaduke Bradley, abbot for three years, as prebendary of Thorpe and residentiary canon. Acts of 1545 and 1547 brought the dissolution of the chantries. There was little resistance - the chantry priests probably pacified by a pension equal to, or higher than, their chantry income.[90] The year 1547 also saw the dissolution of the collegiate church at Ripon. Five ill-educated, poorly paid vicars were appointed to administer the vast parish of Ripon until 1604, when James I re-established the Minster with a dean, sub-dean and six prebendaries, no longer named after districts - Ripon's third ecclesiastical foundation. New arrangements operated for the liberty, especially in criminal cases: the archbishop kept some of his powers; the chapter was permitted a canon fee court for debts and civil matters. At the end of the Civil War the chapter was again dissolved, to be revived at the Restoration.

Traditionally, at the Nunwick Prebend house in 1640, the Treaty of Ripon was signed between commissioners for Charles I and the Scottish Puritans. The treaty, which led to the Long Parliament and to curtailing the power of the monarchy, was to have been signed at York, but the Scots insisted on a different venue and Ripon was chosen.

In 1660 the Minster spire fell. Although apparently still sound, the spires on the western towers were removed for safety four years later. Box pews occupied the choir for some 200 years until the late 1860s.

AN ILLUSTRATED HISTORY OF RIPON

Possibly the most important event to happen since the construction of the present Minster occurred in 1836 when Ripon was chosen as the Cathedral for a new diocese, with Dr Charles Longley as bishop. Ripon was a large diocese: parts of it later formed new dioceses at Wakefield (1888) and Bradford (1920).

A story that the dean and chapter kept the new bishop out of the Cathedral for five years is completely untrue. Longley preached his first sermon in the Cathedral on the 4th December 1836, barely two weeks after his arrival in the city. July 2000 saw the Rt. Revd. John Packer enthroned as bishop to the recently re-styled diocese of Ripon and Leeds.

Under the 1836 foundation, the title 'prebendary' became obsolete. The staff was reduced to a dean and four residentiary canons who lived, during their annual thirteen weeks' duty, firstly at the 'Old' Residence (now the Old Hall) on High St. Agnesgate and from 1859 at the Residence on St. Marysgate. In the 1920s it was decided that the canons should all reside in Ripon.

The former bishop's palace, built 1838-41, chapel added 1848, gave its name to Palace Road. It became a school in 1940. It was converted to housing in the late 1990s after new buildings had been provided for the school in the grounds.

A griffin catches one rabbit whilst another escapes down a rabbit hole. Charles Dodgson (Lewis Carroll) is likely to have been familiar with these carvings. He was visiting Ripon whilst much attention was being focused on the woodwork in the choir in preparation for the restoration by Sir Gilbert Scott.

43

Monastery, Minster, Cathedral

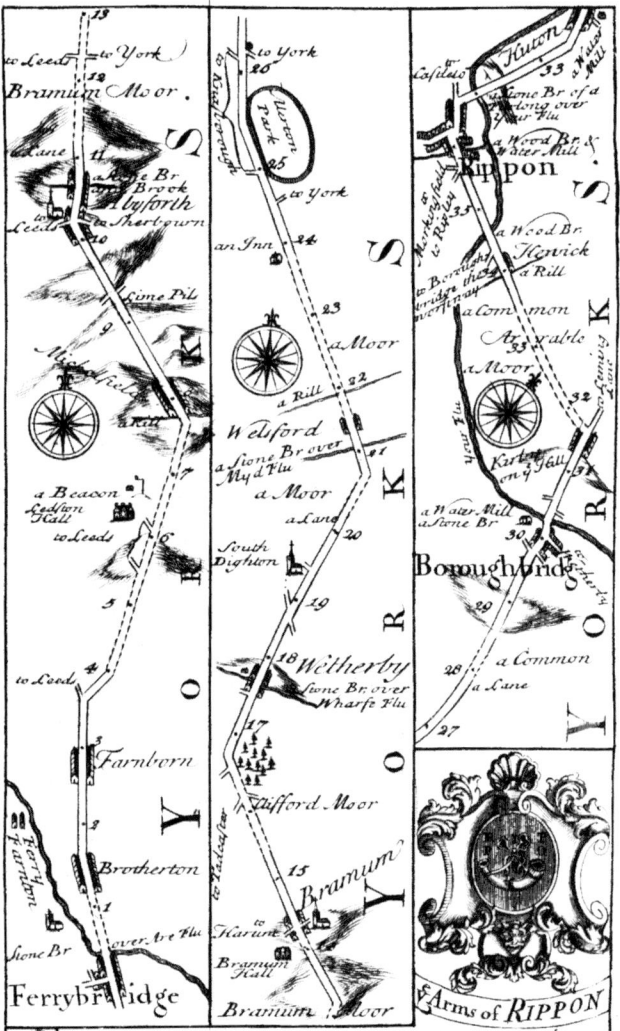

One of the canons was Archdeacon Charles Dodgson, father of Lewis Carroll who, with his family, visited Ripon annually between 1852 and 1868. Carroll would have known the carving in the Cathedral of a griffin catching one rabbit, whilst another escapes down a hole. There are a number of links between his writings and the city.[91] High in the south transept, the Queen of Hearts/ Cheshire Cat corbel acknowledges the connection.

In 1829 there was a restoration of the Cathedral by Blore costing £3,000. In 1854, to celebrate its Cathedral status, new glass was inserted in the east window, followed in the late 1860s by a major restoration under Sir George Gilbert Scott, which cost £30,000. Almost a hundred years later, Archdeacon Graham raised £150,000 for a restoration directed by Sir Albert Richardson; and 1995 saw the end of the latest restoration, costing some £1,500,000, directed by Neil Macfadyen and instigated by Dean Christopher Campling.

The Owen-Bowen map of 1720 includes Ripon.

From 1859 the Residence occupied the site of two former prebendal houses. It was demolished c1970.

Ripon Cathedral from the south east showing the restored stonework.

The growing township

Alma Weir and footbridge 1883. It is difficult to know how long a weir has stood at this point. A weir is first shown here about 1800, but it is possible that from nearby a dam fed a pre-conquest mill at Low Mill. The weir fed water along the mill leat, which ran alongside the wall of Low Mill Road. An arch and the remains of a sluice can still be identified opposite the triangular green at the junction with Priest Lane.

The name Alma commemorates the Crimean War. Thomas Stubbs, formerly Governor of the House of Correction lived at Alma House in his retirement. An enthusiastic collector of Crimean War memorabilia, it was entirely through his efforts that the "Alma" bridge was erected, in 1862. Alma Bridge was popular with early photographers giving fine prospects of the Cathedral. A good number of views, some including the bridge, survive enabling us to identify at least four early 'Alma' bridges.

1st bridge had 2 rails and passing place; 2nd had 3 rails and squarish passing place; 3rd after 1905 had 4 rails and no passing place with Skellfield Terrace complete.

The present Alma Weir was constructed in 1984-5 by Yorkshire Water as part of the scheme to measure the flow of water into the Ouse to assist flood warning for Boroughbridge and York.

Ripon's street pattern is part of its early history. It is generally accepted that the first routes linked the fords across the Skell from the Low Mill/Alma Bridge area to the Ure, passing close to the traditional site of the seventh century Celtic monastery. From this sprang a route to the west, probably Allhallowgate If you stand on North Bridge, about fifty yards (45m) downstream you can see a ford, easily crossed when the river is low and said to be Roman.

The laying out of the market place created a street pattern, still visible today, associated with that new focus of activity.[92] Land was released by the archbishops for building, and burgage, messuage and cottage plots were created.

A burgage was freehold property in a town; a messuage was a tenement (dwelling with its adjoining land). In Ripon, as well as the burgages of the planned borough of the archbishop, there was also the earlier natural borough belonging to the canons of the Minster. Whilst it can be claimed to be too simplistic a view, Professor Jones regarded a messuage belonging to the Minster as equivalent to a burgage within the archbishop's manor. The holder of a burgage (a burgess) had rights and responsibilities, although these were not necessarily all passed down to tenants, particularly the right to vote for members of parliament. Cottages were occupied by bordars and cottars, manorial tenants of low status, usually with little land for their use and few rights. In the thirteenth century, 'moman' was the term used to denote a man who came out of serfdom (slavery) and paid rent for a cottage. The church possessed significant numbers of serfs.

The earliest references to a borough in Ripon that has so far emerged is in the pipe roll for 1194, which records the half-yearly fee of some £36 13s 4d (£36.67) being paid for 'Ripon within the borough'. In 1197 the burgesses owed £10 for having their freedom.

As early as the 1379 Poll Tax, Ripon was divided into four 'wards' or constabularies with 358 taxpayers: Skellgate (36); Westgate (69); Stanbriggate (68); and Marketstede (185). The 1672 Hearth Tax listed: Skellgate (45); Westgate (46); Allhallowgate (97); Crossgate (ie market cross), or Coltsgate Hill (151); a total of 374 taxpaying households. Skellgate ward had most of the better-quality houses, but in Allhallowgate ward there were five houses each with over ten hearths, including one belonging to Sir Edmund Jennings which had fourteen. The wards also probably constituted the districts for the collection of land tax and the election of churchwardens.

The Hearth Tax[93] or 'Chimney money', as this very unpopular tax was also known, was granted by Parliament in 1662 to Charles II *'for the better support of his ... crown and dignity'*. Two instalments of one shilling for every fire-hearth or stove, with certain exceptions for the poor, were collected at Ladyday and Michaelmas each year. Because of widespread evasion in the first two years when the local constables were responsible, special tax collectors were appointed with powers to enter and search. The tax was repealed at the Glorious Revolution in 1688, but the returns give an indication of the more prosperous areas of a town.

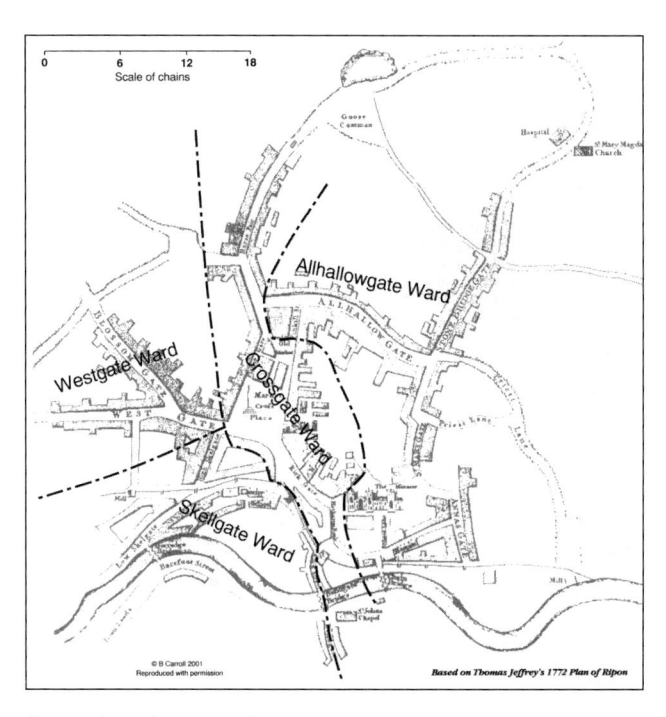

Ripon hearth tax wards.

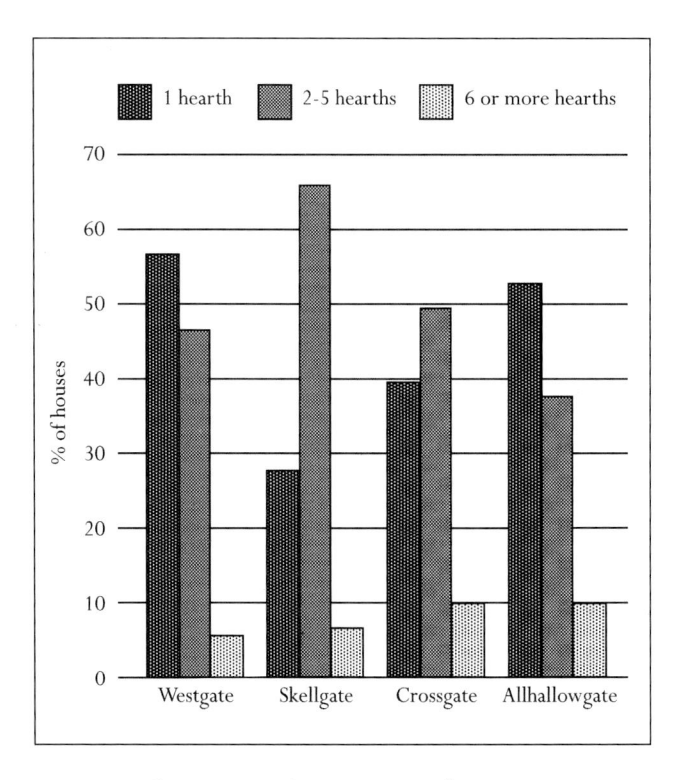

Summary of Ripon Hearth Tax Returns of 1672.

The growing township

It seems likely that Stonebridgegate took its name from North Bridge rather than from the bridge across the open sewer of Skittergate gutter. Stonebridgegate is thought to be 'Herstretegate' - the way of the Saxon host - recorded in the 1360s.[94] The 'host' has been associated with Athelstan's armies on their way to the battle of Brunnanburh. Herstretegate met Allhallowgate near the traditional site of the Celtic monastery, and linked the royal road from Knaresborough to the north. Skelgate - the street leading to the River Skell - is recorded as being owned by the Minster chapter in 1228. High Skellgate appears as Over Skelgate in 1467, which with Nether or Neder Skelgate, Water Skellgate and Skellgarths indicates the route of the Skell through the town. As Leland described it: '... *about this part of the toun Skelle for mille dammes is devidid into 2 partes, and sone after cummith agayn to one botom*'.

Much of Aismunderby, which later largely formed the Hollin Hall Estate, with Bondgate, accommodated the archbishop's bondsmen (serfs/agricultural workers), villein (villagers) and Scandinavian tenants. They had no access for their animals to the Ripon commons until 1461, when they agreed to make annual payments of five shillings to the people of Ripon and five shillings to the master of St. John's Hospital, for access to that part of Bondgate Green south of the Skell. Whilst Bondgate residents were proud of their distinction from Ripon, because of their lack of property qualifications, it was as late as 1823 before even some of the 551 residents could vote in parliamentary elections.

Well before the age of the motor car, the narrowness of Ripon's streets had caused problems. About 1808, ten feet (3m) - to allow room for two carts to pass - was added to the widths of Bedern Bank

The daffodils on the Ripon-Leeds turnpike road were first planted by schoolchildren in 1937. Organised by the Rotary Club, 50,000 daffodil bulbs were planted on the bypass in 1998.

Jeffreys' 1772 map, overlaid with the possible route of the Baronway - Ripon's earliest bypass.

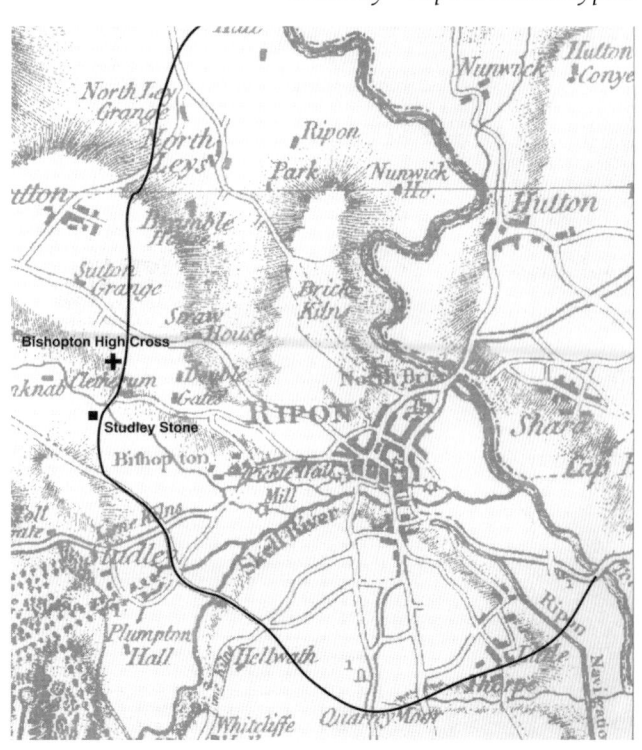

and High Skellgate.⁹⁵ Some early streets have gone altogether - five in the central area alone.⁹⁶ One, from the York Minster Inn (site of the present Boots store), led into Blossomgate; another, east of the town hall, linked Market Place with Water Skellgate at the point where it bridged the millrace.

Travelling to Ripon in 1722, Daniel Defoe described the route from Harewood Bridge as *'a continued waste of black, ill-looking, desolate moors, over which travellers are guided by posts set up for fear of bogs and holes to a town called Ripley'*.⁹⁷ Following the enclosures, new roads had to be created. The main ones were the turnpike roads. Four crossed Ripon's old common land: to Boroughbridge; to Pateley Bridge; and, the first to be turn-piked, to Leeds and Thirsk, an important coaching route now part of the A61. Except where they came within a town boundary, where they had to be repaired by the town, these roads were maintained by the turnpike trusts. The first Ripon trust was set up in 1752, with the Pateley Bridge road being 'piked' by 1756.⁹⁸

In order to ensure that traffic passed through the toll bars, the turnpike trusts forced the closure of what might be called Ripon's earliest bypass, the Baronway. It was recently reported that the stretch of road between Ripon and Ripley had the highest number of road traffic accidents of any stretch of the A61 in North Yorkshire, suggesting a need for improvements along the route.

'Old Boots'. With his boot-jack in one hand and slippers in the other, Wonderful Magazine depicted Tom Crudd, also known as Thomas Spence, 'boot-boy' of the Unicorn Inn. The engraving is dated 1762 but the article did not appear until March 1793: ' it was his business to wait on the travellers who arrived to assist them in taking off their boots...The company in general were so diverted with his odd appearance that they would frequently give him a piece of money, on condition that he held it between his nose and chin. This requisition he was always ready enough to comply with, it being no less satisfactory to himself, than entertaining to them.'

AN ILLUSTRATED HISTORY OF RIPON

The growing township

Severs Fountain. Originally at the junction of Magdalen's Road and North Road, its upper and lower troughs provided drinking water for humans and animals respectively after the commons were enclosed and access to the rivers denied. Without its pinnacle, it now stands in Spa Park.

The principal Ripon coaching inns were the Black Bull and the Unicorn, both still standing in the centre of the city. Although Ripon was not on the main coaching route, for a while the London-Glasgow Royal Mail came via Leeds and joined the Great North Road at Hutton Moor. The Newcastle-London 'Telegraph' coach also stopped, and travellers could catch the 'Tally Ho!' to Leeds. For a trip to the sea at Redcar, a coach left at nine o'clock in the morning.

Ripon was a typical market town, well provided with inns and alehouses: thirty-nine inns and sixteen beer houses were recorded in 1837, offering stabling and refreshment to those who came in from the country, especially on market day. When James Mountain, the owner/driver of the last coach to run regularly between Ripon and Leeds, died in 1856-7, coaches as a means of long-distance public transport had already been forced out of business by the railways. However, the principal inns still retained full stabling facilities. As late as 1900, the Unicorn was preparing to extend its stabling to take 100 horses.

The enclosure of the commons in the nineteenth century not only saw the township increase, but also the financial burden for the upkeep of the new roads. Public carriageways, repairable by the town, were created where routes had crossed the common land. One of these, North Bridge Green Road, is still very much as it was created, apart from the houses. It led from Stammergate to the Ripon-Thirsk road, across North Bridge and followed the line of what we now know as Magdalen's Road and Ure Bank Terrace along the bank of the Ure until the river, which has since changed its course, stopped it. Public foot roads included the Coltsgate Hill and High Common foot road, which can still be walked: from St. Wilfrid's Catholic Church in Coltsgate Hill towards Crescent Road and along 'Killikrankie' to the Masham road across the former High Common.[99] In the late 1870s, North Road, North Street, Kirkgate, Bedern Bank and Cant Lane (off the northern end of Blossomgate) were all widened. The process continued through the twentieth century as Ripon tried to cope with traffic for which its medieval streets were not designed. Taking some ten years, and not completed till 1906, when difficulties over the transfer of the licence of the Grapes were settled, Fishergate was doubled in width. With the Flesh Shambles on its west and Ratten Row on its east, down the length of the present Queen Street stood Middle Street, demolished in 1902-5. At the same time, widening took place at the top of High Skellgate and along part of Westgate. From the late seventeenth century, High Westgate (later Park Street) was developed.

Following the arrival of the railway in the 1840s, Ripon grew northwards; later it spread to the west. After the First World War the site largely occupied by the Army South Camp, along the Harrogate road, was developed for housing. This continued through the century as Ripon's population increased by some fifty percent. The pressure of this burgeoning network of roads, on top of an ever-increasing onslaught of through traffic, made intolerable demands on the medieval heart of the city.

At the rear of numbers 7/8 Park Street, owned by the Baynes family from 1679 to 1791, is a most interesting gazebo. Thought to be of early eighteenth century origin, it was restored in the late 1980s.

The growing township

The first north-south bypass, proposed in 1931, was rejected on the grounds of cost. Further schemes appeared in 1936 and 1947, when much of Bondgate was demolished. The buildings on Bedern Bank followed, and the roundabout was created to take traffic in front of the Cathedral, through Allhallowgate before returning to North Street. In 1960 a proposal for the road to run further west of the Cathedral, cutting through Kirkgate, was reported, but the city council subsequently approved a road to run to the east of the Cathedral, affecting the Cathedral Primary School, Camp Close and Paddy's Park.[100]

January 1970 saw the city council approve a western relief road that swept westwards from Borrage Bridge, via Blossomgate to Coltsgate Hill.[101] This scheme was eventually rejected in favour of an outer bypass, which began to take shape in 1985. Work to the east of the city started in October 1993 and the new road, costing an estimated £16m, came into use on the 11th January 1996, beginning a new era for Ripon.[102] Less than five years earlier, traffic flow had been re-organised to form a through east/west route.

The bypass from the air. Quarry Moor can be seen at bottom left with Morrison's supermarket to the right of the roundabout to the south of Ripon. The bypass is picked up again top right with the double roundabouts and the junction of the A61 with the B6265 Boroughbridge Road along which the canal can be traced.

© *Courtesy of Ripon Gazette*

Ripon's problems with the motor car had been recognised as early as 1897, with a scheme to purchase twenty-four acres (l0ha) to build houses along what became Mallorie Park Drive, to link the traffic from Boroughbridge and Harrogate to the Studley and Pateley Bridge road. Work began in 1902. Three years later, seven motorists were convicted for exceeding the twenty miles (32 km) per hour speed limit on Harrogate Road; several of them went back to see what speed they could clock on the return run. Because of the congested state of Ripon's roads, the magistrates suggested eight miles (13km) per hour on the flat; six on gradients.[103]

The growing township

Earlier, if a town had a navigable river it was prosperous. Without one, prosperity was hard to come by. The nearest navigable point to Ripon was towards Boroughbridge, where heavy goods to and from Ripon would have to be transported. Carters and packhorses followed the mud-tracks which served as roads. A canal to link Ripon to the navigable stretches of the Ure, initially proposed in 1736,[104] was built between 1767-73, at an estimated cost of £8,333, to plans submitted by the Leeds-born designer, John Smeaton. Using thirty-ton barges, the canal took bricks, lead, butter, cheese, corn and agricultural produce, and returned with coal. The toll from Ripon to York was 1s 6d to 3s dependent upon cargo. Seven out of the eight Ripon coal merchants were based at the warehouses around the canal basin, built in 1781. The logo of the Ure Navigation contains a motto which can be translated as 'Ripon, by Divine foresight a harbour'.

The canal was not a financial success. By 1820 it was in debt and in 1847 it was bought by the Leeds and Thirsk Railway Company, later part of the North Eastern Railway Company. They could supply coal from the Durham coalfields cheaper than the canal could transport it from South Yorkshire. Their station-masters were encouraged to act as coal merchants in company time. In 1906, the local stationmaster had a virtual monopoly supplying Ripon's domestic coal trade.[105] By 1894 the canal locks had become inoperable and in 1947 it was declared a 'remainder waterway'.

Ure Navigation Canal Logo - the motto can be translated "Ripon, by Divine foresight a harbour".

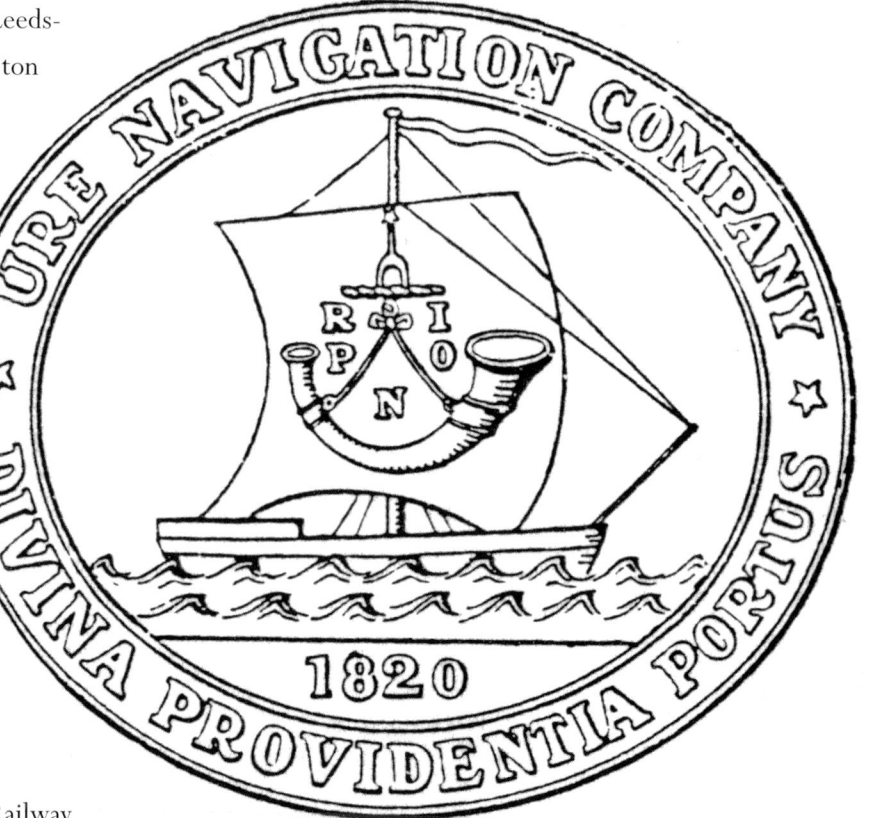

The canal with Ripon Minster in the background (1817).

A northbound mineral train pulled by a wartime 'Austerity 2-8-0 locomotive, crosses the Ure Viaduct immediately south of Ripon Station about 1954 (JW Hague from the DV Beeken collection).

Eight years later the locks at Rhodes Field and Bulfurrow were blown in. From 1982-97 the Ripon Canal Society worked for its restoration, completed as far as the Littlethorpe Road bridge by 1986. An elevated bridge was inserted into the bypass to permit the re-opening of the canal to the basin in 1996. Rebuilding round the canal basin started in 1999.

On the 22nd March 1847, 'The first pile of the railway viaduct over the River Ure, below the North Bridge, Ripon, was driven this day'. Just over a year later the first passenger train travelled from Ripon to Thirsk and back, and on the 14th September 1848 the line opened between Ripon and Harrogate, offering a new prosperity to Ripon. The marquis paid for the planting of the lime trees along North Road to improve the view as his visitors travelled to Studley. There had been debate as to where the railway station should be sited. Bondgate Green, preferred by many, but too close to the Cathedral for others, was not to be. Ure Bank, nearly a mile (1.5km) from the city centre, was selected.

Under the Beeching cuts of the 1960s, the last goods train left Ripon Station for York at 8.30am on the 3rd October 1969. The site was redeveloped for housing in the late 1980s.

The growing township

In 1953 George Jackson counted seventeen bridges in Ripon. Surrounded on three sides by water, it was a natural defence, but for trade and travel, safe crossing points were essential. North Bridge, first mentioned in a document of 1242 and probably the third of Ripon's bridged crossings, contains the earliest surviving masonry in a pointed flood arch on the downstream, southern, bank. The chapel of St. Sitha stood on, or near, the bridge and collected 11s 1d in 1478. Gifts and legacies were received for its repair, the wills of the donors giving insights into its dangerous state and 'great decai'. In 1621, after the settlement of the boundary between the North and West Ridings, it was decided that the bridge belonged to the West Riding and its maintenance became their responsibility. The winter of 1732 saw the bridge extensively damaged by flood, to be rebuilt on its upstream side. Increased traffic followed the arrival of the railway and the bridge was widened in 1879 - from 14 feet 9 inches (5m) to 29 feet 9 inches (9m), at a cost of £7,000.

Bondgate and Hewick bridges are the earliest in Ripon, both being recorded by the twelfth century. Leland, in the 1530s, refers to using a ford beneath Hewick Bridge and wrote: *'There is a faire chapel of freestone on the further ripe of Skell at the very end of Hewick Bridge made by a heremitte that was a mason and it is not full finished.'*

With the dissolution of the chantries a few years later, it seems doubtful if it was ever finished. The chapel of St. Anthony stood at Hewick Bridge by the fifteenth century and collected 5s 3d in 1501. We have Celia Fiennes's eye-witness description of it in 1698:

'There are two good bridges to the town, one was a rebuilding, a pretty large, with severall arches, called Hewet bridge - it's often out of repaire by reason of the force of ye water that swells after great raines; yet I see they made works of wood on purpose to breake the violence of ye streame; and ye middle arche is very large and high.'

The bridge was rebuilt again in the eighteenth century with a span of six arches, and later widened on its upstream side.

Bondgate formed part of the main north-south route via Whitcliffe, Markenfield and Markington to Ripley, or via Bishop Monkton and Burton Leonard to Knaresborough. The Skell was bridged there from about 1100. Money was bequeathed in 1459 for 'Bondgate Brigg', and in 1754 a three-arched stone bridge was built, rebuilt in 1776. In 1892 the present iron bridge was constructed, the watercourse narrowed and the road improved.

From the fourteenth century, possibly earlier, Bishopton Bridge crossed the Laver, providing access to Nidderdale and the west. During the fifteenth century it carried the chapel of St. Mary, and gifts there in 1501 totalled the same as Hewick. By 1522, the chapel was occupied by a hermit. Three years later he had become a 'malefactor', was arrested and taken to York assizes. The road was turnpiked following the Act of 1756 and possibly the upstream part of the bridge dates from that time. In 1885 it was widened from 15 feet (4.5m) to 30 feet (9m) in sandstone, and its approaches were improved with money and land given by the marquis of Ripon. If one looks over the bridge on the upstream side, when the water is low, it is easy to see the remains of a ford.

The sites of Risbrigg (Markenfield/Fountains area) and Gillingbrig ('on the Skell towards the Ure')[106] remain uncertain. Appearing in wills of the fourteenth century, usually with gifts for its repair, the site of Esgatebrigg has not been established with certainty. It has been linked with the first bridge over the Skell after it came within the township, now Borrage Bridge. Borrage derives from burgage, and the bridge enabled the burgesses to reach the far side of Borrage Green, which lay on both sides of the Skell. The bridge was rebuilt in 1765 with the turnpiking of the Thirsk-Leeds road. Following complaints to the West Riding justices about its 'narrow and incommodious state', it was widened on its upstream side in 1885.

'The South-East Prospect of Rippon, in the county of York' 1745 by Buck.

The growing township

Postcards c1900 of the Fairy Steps and the Rustic Bridge.

Before New Bridge, later called Bondgate Green Bridge, was built in 1810, traffic continued down Bedern Bank to just past Thorpe Prebend House, where Chain Bridge spanned the river at Bondgate Green. A ford can still be picked out in the riverbed. The people of Ripon had rights of common on both sides of the river; the millrace continued across the common - sections remain buried in the gardens of the houses on St. Agnesgate. Each year the millrace was to be cleaned out at Whitsuntide by *'persons from Burton Leonard'*,[107] although one wonders, as Burton Leonard was outside the liberty, under what obligation this could have been. Until the early nineteenth century, between the millrace and the river ran a public path known as Bachelor's Walk - perhaps it was a favourite haunt of the young men of the area?

Chain Bridge, alias Archer Bridge, was only a footbridge, so if the ford alongside was impassable, the principal exit east as well as south must have been Bondgate Bridge. Chain Bridge had been built in 1717 by John Aislabie, replacing a wooden bridge of 1480 and can be seen on Buck's view of Ripon (see page 57). However, earlier wills record gifts for the repair of Archer Bridge, so there must have been an even earlier bridge at the site. Aislabie's bridge was dismantled in 1754 and a stone bridge, still only 'convenient for horses and foot passengers', was built by the corporation. Some of the footings can still be seen in the riverbed and one of its ground arches forms the cellars of the present band room. Immediately upstream can still be seen some wooden stakes. These may be the supports of the earlier bridge.

In September 1898 a new wooden bridge, Rustic Bridge, also known as Willows Bridge, was built over the confluence of the Laver and the Skell to Borrage Lane. It was repaired in 1903, after Alderman Wells's child fell through a hole whilst out with her nurse-maid. Fortunately, she was uninjured. The Fairy Steps, a little further upstream, are claimed to have been built during the First World War, but 'man-size' steps appear at this point on earlier postcards. It is more likely that is when the wide side-slopes were added, said to have been to take the wheels of gun carts, with the shallow steps to assist the donkeys as they hauled the carts up the bank.

All in a day's work

The gift of land to the monastery at Ripon in the AD 650s can be roughly compared to thirty or forty farms of some 50 to 120 acres (20-48ha) each. By far the most productive agricultural part of the archbishop's liberty was North Grange, which is likely to have included North Stainley.[108] Ripon Park provided hunting and fishing for the archbishop and his guests.

The rural community worked the land; the townspeople in trades allied to it. Street names such as Horsefair, Cornhill, the Shambles ('butchers' row') and Blossomgate ('plough-swain's way') emphasise the agricultural links. But international wool merchants, a bell founder and a goldsmith were also based in the town. The old corporation managed what could be described as a large communal farm. It was essential to keep the animals off the growing crops, so dates were fixed for their transfer to the waste (cleared woodland), or the fallow. The Towne Book of 1598 is successor to at least three sets of regulations. Many of the rules concern the organisation of this communal farm, eg:

'If any beast strays into the corn or hay fields the fine is 3s 4d. No stoned or scabbed horses allowed on the Common. Geese are only allowed on Rawster Hill. No one may keep sheep on the Ripon commons, on pain of a 4d fine.'

The open-field system frequently created problems from animals straying, and the scattered 'strips' were wasteful of time and labour. Some enclosure had already taken place when, in 1690, the corporation re-allocated the land into better-shaped plots. Having lost the right to graze the stubble after harvest, there was an upsurge of unrest from those who had held 'cattlegates' (the right to pasture an agreed number of animals on the common land). In 1743, a commission decided that the owners of the new plots had to pay an annual sum, the 'average rent', through the mayor to compensate the former holders of the cattlegates. The Towne Book had stated that:

'Any citizen who has and dwells in any mansion house of the ancient yearly rent of 40s or above shall have three gates of the common pasture cattle or horse. Citizens who live in their own mansion houses - 3 gates Those paying rent between 6s 8d and 40s - 2 gates Those paying under 6s 8d rent - one beast gate.'

Ripon was slow to adopt the new husbandry of the eighteenth century. A Board of Agriculture inspection of 1799 revealed that only a quarter of the land was under tillage and artificial grasses were just being introduced. Some short-horned cattle and *'a good many long woollen sheep'* were being bred. Most of the thousands of acres of waste and common in the neighbourhood *'is capable of great improvement'*. Hangovers from feudal land tenure were inhibiting progress.

In 1826, an Act was passed to enclose the only commons then remaining: Ripon Common, Bishopton High Ellers, Bishopton Low Ellers, Sharow Oxclose and Littlethorpe Oxclose. The uneven, 'stinted' pasture of Quarry Moor was not enclosed. (Stinted pasture was where the grazing was limited, for example, by the time of year, or by the number of animals.) At the time of the Act, the grazing rights for the residents of Bondgate were on Quarry Moor, from which Ripon townsmen were excluded. In 1782, Quarry Moor comprised a little over twenty five acres (10ha), of which fourteen were 'greatly damaged' by quarrying. Twenty-four messuage rights and eleven cottage rights were then recorded. The moor was stinted with cattle only, each messuage having two stints and each cottage one.[109] Until 1925, Bondgate had its own pound, or pinfold, standing immediately opposite Bondgate House. In dealing with squatters, if an occupier had been there over twenty years, he or she was granted rights. Commissioner Humphries tried to protect the small landowners, but they could not afford to fence and improve their land, so had little option other than to sell. Miss Lawrence of Studley got the lion's share. Enclosure was not finalised until 1857, when the average rent system, introduced in 1747, was abolished.[110]

With regard to the organisation of the workers themselves, there are occasional references to guilds in the medieval period, e.g. the guild of Corpus Christi, the guild of the Holy Trinity[111] and, about 1406, to the guild of the Holy Cross (or Rood Guild) in whom lands owned by the grammar school were vested. In other towns, merchant guilds are claimed to have pre-Conquest origins. Reference is made to a grant in 1186 to the 'house of the fullers' at Ripon, which seems to imply some kind of amalgamation of craftsmen. However, *'the importance of the guilds depended upon the prosperity of the town and the property which they had accumulated (which in Ripon was probably small), but whatever the value, social or material of the Ripon guilds, they disappeared with those of the rest of England at the time of Edward VI'.*[112]

The Ripon Millenary, published in 1892, covering the events of the 1886 Millenary Festival and the history of the city, takes pains to point out that these guilds were not the trade guilds of later times. Rather, they were those associated with saints and religious mysteries, giving assistance to those in distress, not only to the poor and sick, but also to those who had suffered fire, flood, robbery and even retirement. Unfortunately no records have been found. With such a range of benefits, it might not be unreasonable to see some links with the medieval craft guilds.

As elsewhere, the trading guilds had their own patron saints, e.g. Saint Crispin for shoemakers. They followed their banner in the processions. They made their own rules and, subject to the oversight of an alderman or warden, permitted and controlled those who set up in their craft in the town. The members were not allowed to hawk their wares; could not hire a stranger for more than a month; and took apprentices for seven years - none of whom was allowed to work for a 'stranger' - and was to have left the town before he could set up in business himself.

In 1608 the guilds were formed, or more likely, formalised. They comprised: woollen weavers or clothiers; blacksmiths, locksmiths, spurriers, lorimers (Old French for spurrier) and armourers; saddlers; tailors; merchants and mercers; haberdashers, felt makers and saddlers; tanners; cordiners (shoemakers); glovers, curriers; innholders; butchers; dyers, apothecaries and barber chirurgeons (surgeons).

By 1661, grocers, drapers, joiners, leather dressers, chandlers and bakers had been incorporated into the guilds already in existence, although tailors and tanners still formed separate companies. A rulebook of 1668 of the Company of Drapers, Dyers, Apothecaries and Barber Surgeons is the only one that survives to illustrate the highly-restrictive practices that the guild enforced.

All in a day's work

Ripon's 1379 Poll Tax returns included some thirty eight cloth workers and twenty-five leather workers. Twelve occupations were specified for the prosperous Skellgate ward, but textile and leather trades dominated, with the emphasis on the primary processing of wool and leather, rather than on finished goods. Stonebridgegate ward had ten occupations listed, the most frequent being weaving. One of its five weavers was the well-travelled Lamkynus de Brabant. The eleven occupations in the Westgate district included a hosteler (innkeeper), a cook and three tailors. Marketstead ward, the most populous district, had nearly half of the lay people working in fourteen different trades, amongst which were at least eight shoemakers, three brewers and one barber, as well as over half of the servants taxed in Ripon. Perhaps, not surprisingly, in no other area of the town were there more resident traders, including some of Ripon's wealthiest citizens. The key position of the Marketstead ward in the supply of foodstuffs was indicated by eight butchers. Ecclesiastical uses dominated the south-eastern quarter of Ripon, but the secular world occupied the rest, particularly both market places. About a third of the archbishop's burgages were in the market places. Elsewhere in the town, the messuages of the canons' tenants were more frequent, a situation arising from the dual organisation of the town, evident by 1020 and probably much earlier.[113]

Through the fourteenth century, Ripon merchants exported wool via Hull, and Ripon became the leading cloth town in Yorkshire, producing 1,897 cloths - each one 26 yards by 4 feet 10½ inches (23m x 1.5m) - which was about a third of the 1471-3 county total. Halifax was second with 1,518½ cloths. By 1476, Halifax had overtaken Ripon by some fifty cloths, and by 1479 over a hundred, and so it went on. Ripon cloth was sold at Coney Street, York, together with cloth from Kendal and Knaresborough.[114] It is sometimes suggested that the wool production at Ripon and Fountains Abbey was linked. The Minster canons are thought to have dabbled in the wool trade, but Fountains was the big player and exported much of its wool through Boston in Lincolnshire. Only if Fountains needed to supplement its clip to complete a contract, or for local producers to benefit unofficially from the privileged toll status that many monasteries enjoyed, might local wool have been included with that of the abbey.

Despite the grant of 6s 8d from the Royal Exchequer for 'repairing the house of the fullers at Ripon' in 1186, the archbishop later stopped fulling in Ripon, it is said, to remove competition for his mill at Bishop Monkton, although Bishopton Mill still seems to have continued working. Fulling involved the use of a naturally absorbent clay - fullers earth - which, after heating, was used in the shrinking and pressing of cloth. It was not until the 1340s that fulling was re-established at Ripon,[115] but two centuries later the introduction of new fulling processes from the continent saw the loss, to the West Riding, of traditional Yorkshire cloth production in towns like Ripon, although tanning continued. John Leland wrote in the 1530s:

'There hath bene, hard on the further ripe of Skelle, a great number of tenters for woollen clothes, wont to be made in the toun of Ripon: but now idelnes is sore incresid in the toun and clothe makeing almost decayed.'

Leland made no reference to spur making, but by 1604 Ripon had a national reputation. Sadly, what came quickly went quickly. Ripon's last spurrier, John Terry, died in 1798. His shop, 36 Market Place, now forms part of the Yorkshire Bank site.

Spur making flourished in the seventeenth and eighteenth centuries. It did not make much money for the town or generate a great deal of employment, but 'as true steel as Rippon Rowels' became proverbial and, in Fuller's opinion, 'the best spurs are made at Rippon'. In the seventeenth century a pair of common steel spurs cost ls (5p); a pair of wrought spurs 7s 6d (37½p). The decoration on steel spurs could be embossed or chased, whereas wrought spurs were inlaid, probably with silver. In design and ornamentation they far exceeded any that had preceded them, requiring a very high standard of craftsmanship.[116] When James I visited Ripon, in 1617, he was presented with silver spurs costing £5. It is recorded that he was very pleased with his spurs, and wore them on his departure the next day.

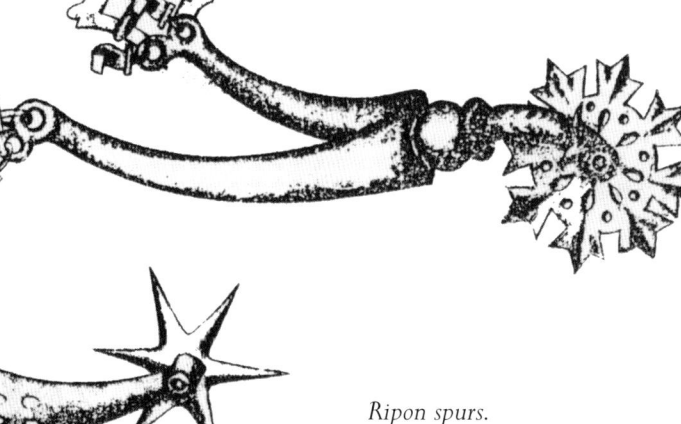

Ripon spurs.

All in a day's work

A 1685 reference in the corporation minutes has *'For Bitts, Buckles, Stirrup irons and spurres, etc. for his grace the Lord Archbishop of York and his attendants 13. 10. 0d'*. There is a tradition that a century later no traveller could pass through Ripon without having his spurs taken away and having to pay to get them back. Buckles here appears to relate to harness, but on Easter Day the young men would take the buckles from the girls' shoes and on Easter Monday the girls would take the men's. Although the town did not gain the reputation for buckles that it did for spurs, buckles made in Ripon survive.

About this time, bone-lace making is mentioned in Ripon. On the 23rd November 1629, in addition to asking for a fulling mill, the mayor and the aldermen petitioned the archbishop of York to ask the king to allow a house of correction to be established in the town, at which the poor, unemployed people could make bone lace, Manchester

The charter horn. Notice that, in the centre, a crossbow hangs alongside the spur. There may be a link between Ripon's medieval crossbow makers and the later development of specialist spur making in the town.

Buckles thought to have been made by the Ripon spurrier John Terry about 1770.

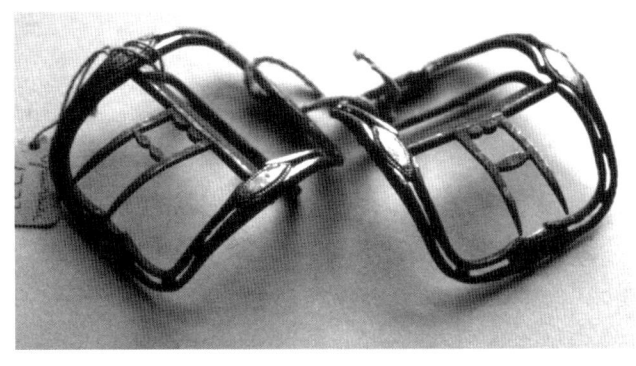

Young ladies show off saddletrees at the 1896 Festival.

wares' and coarse woollen cloth. The first Ripon bone-lace worker we know about is Alice Teasdill, from her will of 1635. Because Yorkshire lace is very similar to Lille lace, it has been suggested that lace making was brought to England by Protestant girls sent to France to be educated. Ripon lace developed its own patterns, adding detail not used in the Point de Lille.[117] Blossomgate and Bondgate were the areas most closely associated with lace making. Bondgate was also the focus for the manufacture of saddletrees, the frames around which saddles were built.

In the 1850s, Thomas Walker and Robert Aslin, wholesale lace merchants, were still in business in Ripon, but by 1862 the cottage industry had collapsed in the face of competition from machine lace, and there was only one lace maker left.[118] In 1912, in an effort to keep the craft alive, lace making classes were being organised.

Garnett's burling and mending rooms (removing and repairing the small knots, or lumps, from cloth) operated in Bondgate into the l980s. In 1956, the Ure Bank Bobbin Mill closed - 'the last relic of the medieval economy'. It had opened in 1883 making wooden bobbins. The site was sold to Allton's Steel. Close to it stood the malt kilns. Some buildings remain at Ure Bank, but nothing survives of the malt kilns that stood opposite The Crescent on North Street, and there is very little to identify other malt kilns that were scattered around the city. In 1822, seven maltsters were at work in Ripon; three were also brewers.

All in a day's work

Varnish making at Williamson's, 1956.

If a French connection is possible for Ripon's bonelace production, it is a certainty for its varnish industry. Having a smattering of French, Daniel Williamson, a private banker, befriended a refugee from the French Revolution who had found his way to Ripon. In return for this kindness, and the hospitality offered, Williamson was to learn the secrets of varnish making. At first only a hobby, the downfall of the private banks encouraged Mr Williamson to take up varnish making for profit. In 1775 a new industry began in Ripon, eventually to make it the first 'city of varnish' in the country. The site near Borrage Bridge, which Riponians still associate with Williamson's, previously Skin Yard, was not acquired until the twentieth century; their earlier works was further downstream. They moved to Stonebridgegate in 1985.

The Kearsley family was not only involved with varnish. In 1826, Henry Kearsley established the British Iron and Implement Works on North Street, adding warehouses on Trinity Lane. Their implements won international awards. With a staff of about a hundred, the company was Ripon's largest employer, but by the 1890s *'the trade of Ripon is almost nil.'* [119] Despite the general poverty, Kearsley's employees' 1906 annual outing was a forty-eight hour trip to Paris. The foundry ceased working in 1929; the chimney, a familiar landmark, was demolished in 1952. There were other foundries at Bondgate Green and Kirkgate. J.Ingram's Kirkgate foundry was established before Kearsley's, on Skellgarths. An example of their work can be seen in the milepost on the Ripon side of Ripley.

Until 1547, six water mills paid tithes to Ripon Minster: Hutton, Studley, Winksley, Aldfield, Markington, and Givendale near Newby Hall. The right to a mill was an extremely valuable concession. Mills were usually leased with the privilege of multure, obliging tenants to have their corn ground there. Multure was always unpoplar, and the archbishop's officers would search out and smash the hand-mills used by the tenants to avoid the often extortionate tolls. The system operated until the nineteenth century.

The Domesday Book of 1086 records one mill at Ripon. This was probably East Mill, or Low Mill, mentioned as early as 1221. Its successor stood until 1938. A sluice fed a later additional mill which processed timber and bones.

If Low Mill was the first mill, the second mill to be established in Ripon would be the town mill, or Byemill. The name suggests it appeared after the new town had been laid out. It is first mentioned in 1228. There is an early eighteenth-century reference to Duck Hill Mill as Byemilne. For most of its life Duck Hill Mill was a corn mill, but in the eighteenth century an engine was installed to pump water up to the town, and for a short while in the 1790s it worked cotton.

The Old Low Mill, demolished 1938, showing the mill race - Jim Gott (Courtesy of Kelvin Gott).

All in a day's work

After the collapse of High Cleugh Dam in 1892, the corporation purchased Duck Hill Mill from the Ecclesiastical Commissioners for £400 so that seventy square yards (65m^2) of the site could be used for road widening. The building was re-modelled; a steam engine drove the wheel until 1957, when the mill was put up for auction, but then withdrawn. It continued producing animal feed for some years, but in 1988 was converted into dwellings. Five years later the east-west bypass completed the road widening.

The millrace, extremely long for so early a construction, ran from a dam at High Cleugh, and crossed Borrage Green Common (remains can be found in the gardens of Mallorie Park Drive). Nine feet (3m) wide and twelve feet (3.5m) deep, it flowed down Somerset Row, Water Skellgate and Skellgarths, returning to the river near Bondgate Green Bridge.

Above top: Duck Hill Mill (G Fossick).

Above middle: High Mill stood at the foot of Firby Lane. The wall to the right was demolished during the road widenning of 1988.

Above bottom: High Cleugh -a watercolour by George Jackson c1948.

Left: Water Skellgate the old Jepson's Hospital. Four bridges spanned the mill-race as it passed between High Mill and Duck Hill Mill. Culverting took place in 1875.

However, well into the eighteenth century it continued along Bondgate Green Common - substantial arched-over remains exist in some of the gardens on High St. Agnesgate - and along Low Mill Road to Low Mill, before returning to the Skell. In the nineteenth century the weir at High Cleugh had already been washed away three times, to be repaired largely at the expense of the owner of High Mill. After forty hours of continuous rain, on the 15th October 1892, it collapsed, never to be replaced. In 1948, stakes and masonry from the dam could still be seen in the riverbed at a time when Riponians were getting used to the new concrete embankments and breakwaters.

In the 1850s, Cobhams steam mill in Bondgate was established, with another at Ure Bank. Fifty times more efficient, steam mills had been making life difficult for water mills for some time, and after the destruction of the dam at High Cleugh, High Mill and Union Mill closed down.

Reference has already been made to the likelihood of there having been a fulling mill at Ripon in 1186. Another name for a fuller was 'walker' - from 'walking' or trampling the cloth during the fulling process - and an alternative name for the fulling mill was the walk mill. Le Walke Milne Bank was the earlier name for Bedern Bank, at the bottom of which stood New Mill - as it was called in 1643 - more or less where the roundabout is now, where the millrace emerged from Skellgarths (Millgate) before continuing along St. Agnesgate. Walk Mill is its likely predecessor. Rebuilt as a corn mill in the eighteenth and nineteenth centuries and known as Union Mill, it was demolished during the First World War, its rubble providing hard-core for the roads of the army camp.

Union Mill about 1905.

All in a day's work

The third of Ripon's mills, High Mill - or West Mill - was in existence by 1500. It stood on Skellbank at the bottom of Firby Lane, extending in front of Hugh Ripley Hall (built in 1914 as the drill hall). The mill was demolished for road widening in 1902. Two of its millstones are preserved in the entrance to Hugh Ripley Hall. At the end of the eighteenth century the mill ran twenty-four hours a day; one shift milling corn and the other, using water from St. Wilfrid's Well, making paper. At much the same time, for a few years, High Mill, Duck Hill Mill and Bishopton Mill were working cotton.

A mill is recorded at Bishopton by 1305, belonging to the archbishop. In 1531, when Ripon's cloth industry was in decline, it is referred to as Bishopton Walk-myll, a fulling mill, and it was subsequently converted to a corn mill.[120] Bishopton Flax Mill was added in 1792. Its rope-walk is shown on the nineteenth-century maps. In the late nineteenth and early twentieth centuries it was working timber. As it drew water via an aqueduct from higher up the Laver, it survived the destruction of High Cleugh Dam. Extensive structural improvements were completed in 1896; new machinery was added and electric light installed. Its rope-walk was power driven. In 1906, the mill owners were engaged in refuting allegations of very low wages, and the same year Christopher Jeffrey, aged sixteen, had to have an arm amputated after it caught in a carding machine. In June 1915, Bishopton Hemp and Tow Spinning Mill was destroyed in a spectacular fire with the loss of sixty jobs, mostly for women and girls. How many responded to an advertisement in the local newspaper the following week, for flax and hemp workers in Bristol, is not known.

Bishopton Corn Mill.

Ripon in 1772 from a plan by Thomas Jeffreys. Notice the line of the mill stream from the west near High Mill until, having powered the wheels of Duck Hill Mill, and Union Mill the water returns to the Skell at Low (East) Mill. Notice also the bridges, without which it was almost impossible to cross.

71

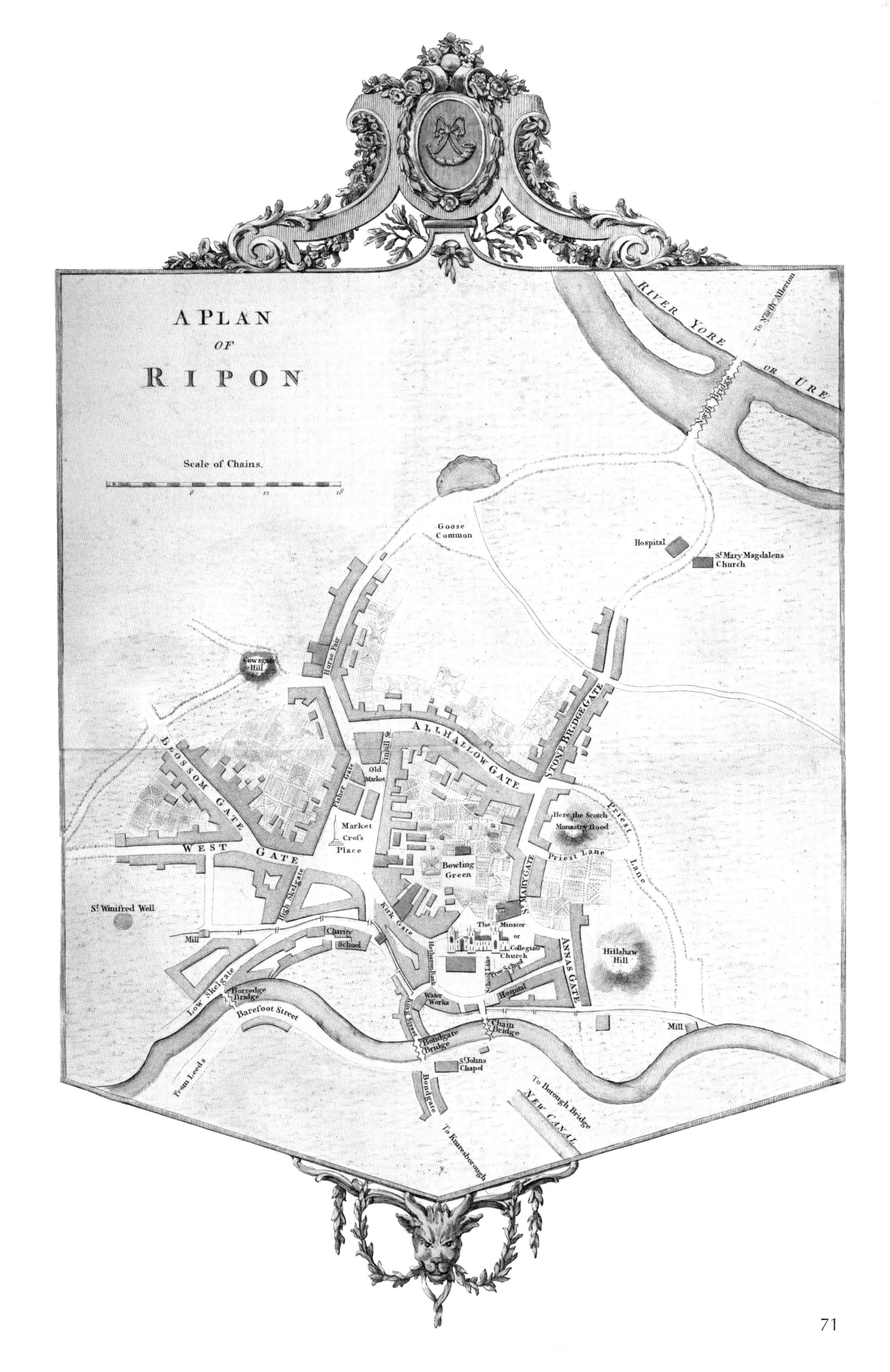

Civic pride

The bathing pavilion on the River Ure was in use from the 1890s to 1951.

Boating on the River Ure upstream of the old boating station.

Because of its situation in an angle formed by the rivers Ure and Skell, water has been an important factor in Ripon's development. Crossing points - initially fords, later bridges - were essential. For most of the year, the Skell supplied sufficient water to drive four mills as it passed through the town.

From 1776, for almost 100 years, water was pumped from the medieval millrace at Duck Hill Mill to standpipes in the town, initially through elm pipes, later lead and, after 1855, iron. Earlier, it was carted in leather bags and sold to the townspeople, but it is clear that for centuries contamination of the waterways had been of increasing concern, so much so that inspectors were appointed in the late fifteenth and early sixteenth centuries. Water Skellgate, Nether Skelgate and Skellgarths - the area where the tanners and cloth workers would be found - receive particular mention, and fines for washing hides, 'lyme skynes', a 'natbagg' and for leading an ox-wagon of dung through the water are recorded.

Nine bridges spanned the millrace. The ducks on the millpond, which practically filled the road at Duck Hill Mill, are said to have given the hill its name. As far as is known, there was no ducking stool in Ripon. Instead, as at his manor at Otley, the archbishop had a 'cucking' stool (as in cuckold) on which offenders were exposed to public humiliation, sometimes outside their own homes. The millrace along Skellgarths was arched over by 1832, and along Water Skellgate in 1875. It has been dry since High Cleugh Dam last burst in 1892.

Ripon's rivers have long brought pleasure and pain. The Ure rises quickly and its currents have claimed many lives. Great floods have been recorded. In 1869, the master of the York and Ainsty hunt, three huntsmen, two ferrymen and nine horses drowned whilst crossing the swollen river at Newby. To avoid the flood plain, buildings were generally constructed above the seventy-five foot (25m) contour.

In an attempt to improve the purity, but more especially the regularity, of the domestic water supply, the corporation installed a steam pump on the Ure, transferring some 300,000 gallons (1.4 million litres) a day to a reservoir along Little Harries Lane at Lark Hill. The new system came into use in 1865, but complaints about the quality of the water soon followed, until a scheme for a gravitational feed from Lumley Moor, in 1888, brought a regular supply of water through the hydrants. The small area of land by the redundant pumping station became the boating station; the Atrium Leisure Club now operates from the pumping station site.

To reduce the number of drownings, a bathing pavilion, for males only, opened on the Ure in 1890. Dean Fremantle had offered to build swimming baths costing up to £400 on the corporation land at Skellbank. Unfortunately, when the plans were drawn, the cost considerably exceeded that sum, but the money was re-offered towards the cost of the corporation erecting the baths. Further plans were drawn up for public baths in Park Street, but that also was too expensive. As a compromise, a bathing pavilion, at a safe section of the Ure, was suggested and the dean agreed to contribute his £400. There was a caretaker's house and twenty cubicles open for five months of the year. The charge, which included towel and costume, was one penny. In August 1899, the sixth annual sports of the Ripon City Swimming Club were held there. The pavilion proved very popular, and at one time the scene was described as 'like a sea front'. It was demolished in 1951, but the site can still be identified from the brick wall along the south bank of the Ure above North Bridge.

To prevent promiscuous bathing from the other bank, approval was given for Sunday opening between 7am and 6pm in 1913, and a byelaw was introduced to prohibit bathing other than at the pavilion. But public bathing remained a male-only activity; in 1917 an application for mixed bathing was refused.

Three years earlier, another proposal for a swimming pool in the Spa Gardens had been postponed, but in 1919 a scheme was drawn up by a Canadian army officer to construct a miniature lake at High Cleugh. The military offered to provide the labour if the city council would meet the £20 cost of materials. The Canadian troops left before the work could be done and the project was abandoned. It was not until 1936 that a public swimming bath was incorporated into the Spa complex.

On the 25th April 1933 a meeting was held at the Lawrence Hotel, when it was resolved that a new swimming club be formed in Ripon, and that the club be called the Ripon Swimming Club. Having decided that five shillings per member demanded by Mr Duffield for use of the bathing pavilion was too expensive, negotiations were in hand to rent a stretch of river in the field beyond the pavilion from Mr Johnson of High Common Farm at £3 for the first year, and £4 thereafter. However, the following month it was unanimously decided to accept Mr Duffield's offer:

'to fence off the portion of land at the end of the Bathing Pavilion for the sole use of the club, to erect a landing stage, and allow the Club to use the large end dressing hut, at a charge of 3s 6d per head (excluding Sundays), the Club to erect one hut for the use of the ladies'.

AN ILLUSTRATED HISTORY OF RIPON

Civic pride

The Spa was a belated attempt to boost Ripon's economy. From 1760, people had been receiving benefit from a sulphur well in Spa Field, Stonebridgegate - the capped well stands close to the line of Skittergate Gutter, by the boundary of the gas holder site and Williamson's (the old gasworks site) - but a scheme to pipe sulphur water from Aldfield to Park Street was chosen.
In 1900, the marquis of Ripon sold the drill field for a pump room and spa, the gardens of which were laid out in 1902. The bandstand followed a year later and, against much opposition, Sunday concerts were presented from 1905. Park Street and Studley Road were widened, requiring the demolition of Pickle Hall, Avenue House and the old museum. Samuel Stead designed the art nouveau Spa Baths which opened in 1905, the year Sir Christopher Furness of Grantley Hall bought Elmcroft for the Fountains - later the Spa Hotel, which opened in 1909.

Ripon's policemen stand ready to prevent trouble whilst the band played on in the Spa Gardens.

Skellbank public bathhouse (built c1810, demolished May 1935). In 1890 a new boiler was installed and the cost of a hot bath reduced from 1s (5p) to 4d (1½ p).

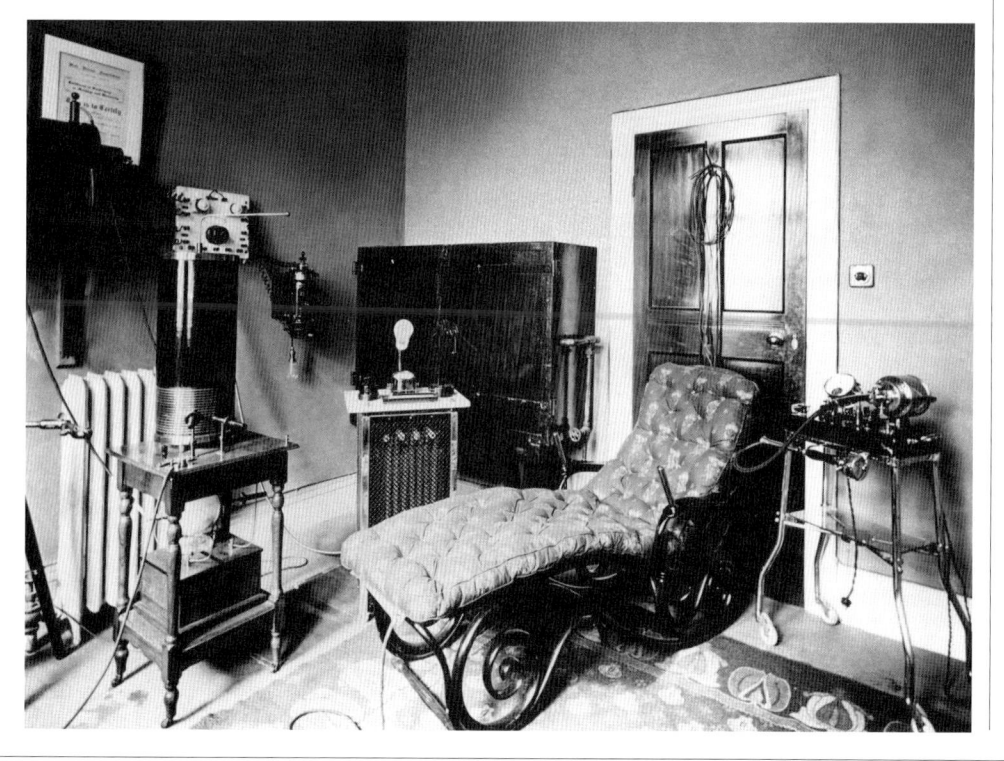

Doctors' bath room for electrical treatment, Ripon Spa.

The exterior of the Spa Baths c1915 after the arrival of the statue of the Marquis of Ripon and the Spa Hotel.

Reflecting the depressed economy some three years later, along with the Unicorn, the Spa Hotel went up for auction, but no bids were received. The fashion for spa treatments had passed and the scheme never achieved its potential. It closed in 1947 after the corporation learned that a year's takings at Ripon were less than a day's at Harrogate Spa.[121]

In 1854, Ripon was alarmed by a number of deaths from cholera in Allhallowgate, blamed by the medical officer on poor sanitation and the fact that the water supply system could not cope, flowing for only a short time once a day. A new sewer laid in the market place in 1851 was too shallow to drain all the cellars: *'the passage of the filth [is] extremely sluggish. The consequence is that ... the stench from the open gratings is not only offensive to passers by, but injurious to the health of the families occupying the contiguous houses'*. Other drains were reported as being too small, at insufficient depth, or without enough 'fall' for the effluent to disperse. The Board of Highways disclaimed responsibility, saying that its duty was merely to surface drainage. The introduction of water closets had produced ever greater quantities of sewage. Watercourses, especially Skittergate Gutter and the Skell, were open sewers described as *'a disgrace to a civilised community'*.[122]

Civic pride

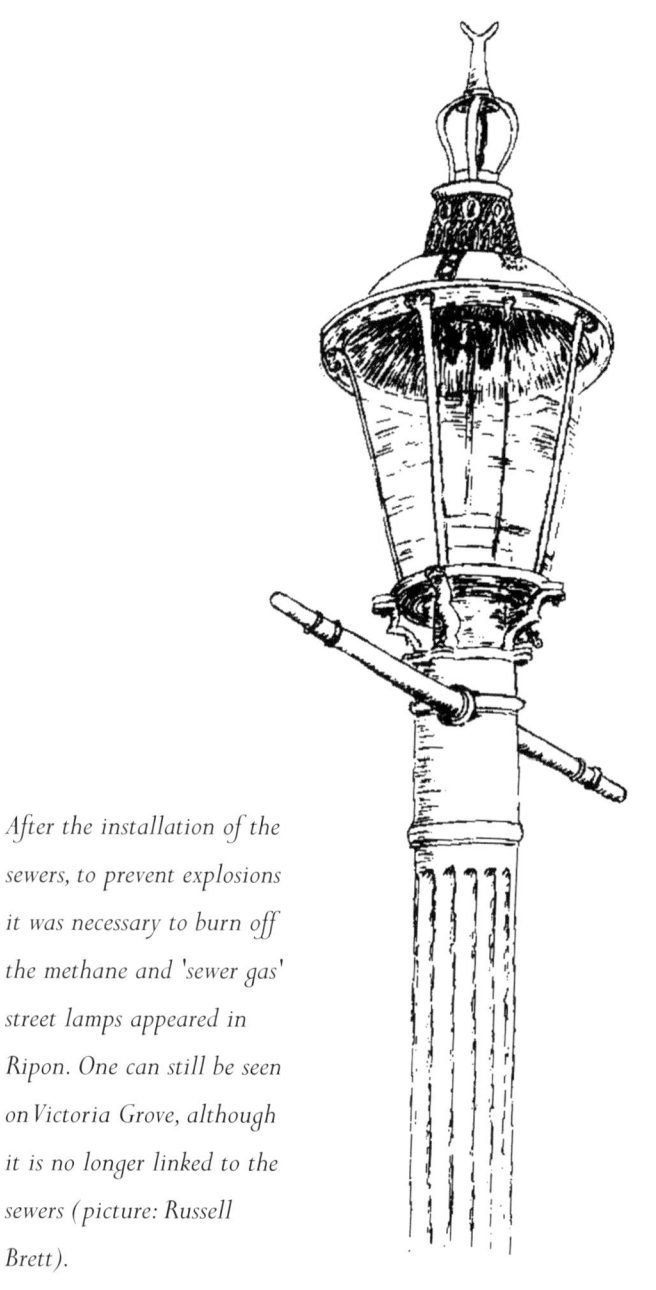

After the installation of the sewers, to prevent explosions it was necessary to burn off the methane and 'sewer gas' street lamps appeared in Ripon. One can still be seen on Victoria Grove, although it is no longer linked to the sewers (picture: Russell Brett).

After having concentrated resources on improving the water supply, in 1879 a sewage works was proposed. The plan began to move forward in 1892 when the council considered a scheme for drainage and sewage disposal costing £17,000. Drains and pipes were laid, and in October 1896 the sewage works at Fisher Green officially opened. Cases of dysentery, typhoid, typhus and cholera fell dramatically.

Having previously been lit by oil lamps, from 1830 the town and the Minster converted to gas. Until 1863, the Studley Estate paid £25 a year towards the cost of Ripon's street lighting. The stone crosses around the Obelisk were replaced in 1882 by six Brays gas lamps, which were themselves replaced by the gas company in 1899 with four of the more economical Kitson oil lamps, one at each corner of the market place. The Brays lamps were to be used elsewhere.

From 1890, Studley Royal House was lit by electricity. Six years later Bishopton Mill followed, as did the Spa Hotel when it opened in 1909. The army camp had its own generating station and made an offer to the corporation to supply the town from the same station, but the offer was not taken up, on the grounds that once the troops had gone there would be little demand for this form of energy. In 1929, a public electricity supply was switched on, the Cathedral converting two years later.

In 1869, permission was granted to erect telegraph lines through the city. The first post office in Ripon was at Wm Farrer, booksellers, 21 Market Place, from 1805. The building is now demolished, but stood next to Thomas the Bakers on the corner of Fishergate. The year 1840 saw the arrival of the first two-horse mail coach from York and the transport of northern letters to Carlton Station on the Great North Railway. From 1857 until 1891 the post office was in Kirkgate, after which it moved to 37 Market Place, then to the other side of the town hall, 39 Market Place. In April 1891, permission to carry telephone wires through Ripon on wooden posts was granted, and on the 1st June 1892 'telephonic communication opened with towns in Yorkshire' from the telegraph office at 35 Market Place.

Land was purchased on North Street in 1905 for a new post office. In 1957 the Post Office took over the building on Finkle Street, which had been the Mechanics Institute from 1892 to 1927, then the Customs and Excise office, but the sorting office stayed at North Street until 1968. The year 1972 saw the last mail with the 'Ripon' postmark, except for a commemorative cover on the 17th June 1986.

Market place c1830.

Fun and games

The St. Wilfrid Procession: Mrs Ada Burton offering Wilfra Tarts.

Wilfra Tarts
Pastry
6oz (180g) plain flour
3oz (90g) soft margarine
1oz (30g) caster sugar
1 egg.

Place the ingredients in a bowl and, using a fork, mix to form a firm dough. Knead lightly, turn out and use to line twelve bun tins.

Filling
1 small lemon; 1 large slice of white bread (in pieces); 2oz (60g) butter (in small pieces); ¼ pint of milk; 1oz (30g,) ground almonds; almond essence; 1 level tablespoon caster sugar; 2 eggs (lightly beaten) Put butter, bread and lemon rind in a bowl. Heat the milk and pour this over the bread, mixing well. Add the other ingredients and use to fill the pastry cases.

Cooking
Bake at 350°F/180°C/gas mark 4 for 25-30 minutes.

Ripon abounds in customs and traditions, and it is difficult to know what to leave out. With such a diversity of events and gatherings on which to draw, this account only scratches the surface. Most often seen are the hornblower, setting the watch, and the bellman ringing for the start of the old corn market, already mentioned in earlier chapters.

Another well-reported custom is that of housewarmings. On midsummer eve, after moving to a new neighbourhood, bread, cheese and ale would be laid before the door for those who chose to partake. In 1823, this was remembered as a 'custom from time immemorial'.[123] If the master of the house was 'of ability', then the neighbours would be invited in for supper. Into the twentieth century Wilfra tarts, Ripon spice bread, or Ripon apple cake (a pie with apple and cheese inside), were placed at doors for passers-by during St. Wilfrid's Feast, especially along the processional route. It has been kept alive by Mrs. Ada Burton presenting jam tarts as the procession passes along Southgate.

A custom still performed is 'seeking the mayor'. The role of first citizen is not always easy and can be costly. In earlier days, some nominees hid. Similar to the election of the Speaker of the House of Commons, in Ripon seeking the mayor became formalised into a feigned reluctance to take the office, with the mayoral sponsors performing a ritual search.

To distinguish the house of the mayor, in 1892 a special lamp was purchased. Seven years later, the lamp standard outside Green Royd, Studley Road, the residence of mayor Arthur Wells, moved with the lamp. Appropriately, the mayor's lamp was the first street light to be restored following the withdrawal of blackout regulations after World War II.

Prior to 1847, on St. Wilfrid's Feast, then held in the middle of August, an effigy of the saint, described either as wearing cocked hat and black coat, or full-sized, wigged, booted and spurred, was paraded around the city by increasingly intoxicated attendants and musicians. With coins from adults, youngsters were encouraged to shake hands with him and cheer. Races followed, each area of the city organising its own on succeeding evenings. On the Sunday and Monday, the pleasure grounds at Studley Royal were open free of charge to the general public and great crowds flocked to Ripon on special trains for the celebrations.

Various explanations have been given for the origin of the Wilfrid Procession: the people greeting Wilfrid on his return from exile; the great feast and procession of kings and prelates on the consecration of the abbey church; or the procession of monks and townspeople who met the cortege when Wilfrid's body returned to Ripon for burial. Most likely it goes back to the early thirteenth-century processions to display the splendid new shrine of St. Wilfrid and the richly decorated feretory, a portable shrine containing his skull. During the medieval period, each year, three great feasts were devoted to St. Wilfrid in Ripon: the 24th April, the 'translation' of his bones; the Sunday after Lammas (the 1st August), to celebrate his birth; and the 12th October, to remember his death. The *'Office of St. Wilfrid according to the use of Ripon'* 1833 has 4th October as the deposition or death of St. Wilfrid. Most of Ripon's customs had been discontinued by 1830. Whit Sunday-school processions may have restored something of what the people missed, and it seems likely that the townsfolk were organising their own St. Wilfrid's Feast, the effigy of the saint taking the place of the shrine.

Preceded by a couple of musicians the effigy of St. Wilfrid is led along Kirkgate. With an account of the procession this illustration appeared in the Illustrated London News of 1844.

Fun and games

Nineteenth century racing at Ure Bank.

Horse racing is first mentioned in Ripon in 1664 when Matthew Townley, watching a race on Bondgate Green, fell whilst dismantling the spires on the Minster. One cannot infer a race meeting from this, but in 1675 and 1692 organised racing did take place on Monkton Moor, followed by a horse fair. In 1713, the corporation ordered a racecourse to be made on High Common. Racing started - one meeting a year - in 1717. The Aislabies of Studley Royal were early supporters, and

Mrs. Aislabie caused a scandal by sponsoring at Ripon what is thought to be the earliest ladies' horse race in the country, when *'nine of that sex rid astride, dress'd in drawers, waistcoats and jockey caps, their shapes transparent, and a vast concourse to see them'*.[124] Although horse fairs continued, following the enclosure of the commons, horse racing stopped in 1826.

Some ten years later: *'Mr Haygarth, a publican got up some races on a small scale, in his own fields, which roused the old sporting spirit of the town, and induced several respectable individuals to form themselves into a committee, when a race course was formed and a stand erected on the north side of the river Yore.'*[125]

Race Course Road was an earlier name for Ure Bank Terrace. Races were held on this course from 1837 until 1865, when a new course was laid out off Whitcliffe Lane, but that proved dangerous. A new company was formed in 1880, with yet another in 1898, which two years later moved the racing to Boroughbridge Road.

In the 1840s the races, one two-day meeting a year, were linked to St. Wilfrid's Feast, then held at 'Old Lammas' in the middle of August. However, in 1847 the race committee moved the races, and the feast, two weeks earlier to the Sunday after the 1st August (Lammas), and presented their own effigy of St. Wilfrid wearing mitre and priestly costume.[126] There were protests over the change of date and garments, with a second Wilfrid appearing a fortnight later for about three years, but the move continued until it was tied in with a public holiday introduced on the first Monday in August and, coincidentally, with the date in the James II charter. That holiday was moved to the end of August, but now, on the Saturday before the first Monday in August, a human Wilfrid, dressed as both abbot and bishop, parades the streets of the city. In 1996 the Cathedral re-introduced a Wilfrid Procession and festival in October.

Wilfrid procession.

St. Wilfrid's 'Feast' was given a new lease of life in 1962. A committee was formed and a tail of floats added to the original procession which, each year, with 'Abbot Wilfrid' at its head, starts its journey round the city - said to symbolise his journey to Rome (more accurately Compiègne, France) for his consecration as bishop of Northumbria. On reaching St. Wilfrid's RC Church he moves to the end of the procession, and continues as 'Bishop Wilfrid', in which role he is greeted by the dean and symbolically led to the bishop's chair in the Cathedral. Older Riponians remember his being affectionately called 'Daddy Wilfra' in the earlier years of the twentieth century, and his feast day 'Wilfra Day'.[127]

Fun and games

Each night at nine o'clock at the four corners of the Obelisk, the hornblower ceremonially sets the watch. Ripon is unique in such a custom, and on a warm summer evening a large crowd gathers to listen as the mournful tones echo around the market place. How long since it began is difficult to say - certainly from the medieval period. The horn is now blown four times at the Obelisk, followed by three times at the mayor's house. In the eighteenth century it was blown three times at the mayor's house followed by three times at the Obelisk. When the mayor lived an unreasonable distance from the market place, the precedent of blowing the horn at the town hall steps and afterwards at the Obelisk had been established.

Simultaneously with the hornblowing, the curfew bell tolls automatically thirty times from the southwest tower of the Cathedral, formerly warning citizens to stay in their houses till dawn. Suspicion fell on anyone the constables found abroad at night.

Signalling the need to be shriven - to make one's confession and receive absolution - before Lent began, on Shrove Tuesday the bell on the central tower rang out as the 'pancake bell', from the custom of eating up the foods forbidden in Lent. The ringing of the pancake bell had lapsed by the early twentieth century, when the same bell was rung at two-thirty for the afternoon service and was then referred to as both the sermon bell and the sanctus bell. It was re-cast in 1964, and is now rung as the service bell. Fifty times, the ninth bell in the south-west tower now rings as the pancake bell at eleven o'clock on Shrove Tuesday morning.

In the medieval period the bells were hung in the north-west tower, and from there the 'great bell', Klank Knoll, sombrely rang out for deaths and funerals from at least 1379 to 1762.[128] Until World War II, a 'passing bell' rang: nine for a man, six for a woman, and three for a child followed by one for each year of the child's age.

The last record of the Sin Eater in this area, a dirty, old man with tangled hair who, for a payment, took upon himself the sins of the deceased, was at Sharow in the late nineteenth century.[129] Only permitted into a house of death, he would be taken to the room where the deceased lay, to stand on one side of the body whilst the next of kin stood opposite. On the chest of the loved one would have been placed a piece of bread and a tankard of ale, containing half-a-crown (12½ p). The Sin Eater would take the bread, saying *'With this bread I take upon me the sins of…'* naming the deceased. He would then take up the tankard and, making sure he gathered the coin as he drank, would intone, *'With this ale I take upon me the sins of…'.* With a strong stick, the next of kin would then drive the Sin Eater from the house.

At Ripon died the only North Yorkshire woman thought to have lost her life because of witchcraft:

'Mary Milner of Ripon this day Friday 1st June 1821 did tell me (she having a good memory of it) that in April 1764 (she in her 10th year) one Master Ogle who did commonly smell witches, on that night smelled one to her death'.[130]

Since the laws against witchcraft had been repealed in 1736, this woman's death must have been the result of mob violence.[131]

Still to be heard in the Cathedral are prayers for the dead, called the 'Year's Mind'. In earlier days this formed part of the 'bidding of bedes' (prayers) when a full procession passed through the graveyard and a long list of bidding bedes was read.

At Candlemas the medieval church held ceremonies, including the carrying of hallowed candles, which continued at Ripon into the eighteenth century. On the Sunday before Candlemas Day, the 2nd February, the Minster church at Ripon was reported as being *'one continual blaze of light all the afternoon by an immense number of candles'*.[132] The ceremony was revived in 1964, and is very popular.[133]

The Cathedral set for Candlemas (photo Robert Lambie).

Fun and games

The seventh century crypt (St.Wilfrid's needle) In the medieval period it became the custom, as a test of purity for a young woman prior to marriage, 'to pass through the eye of St. Wilfrid's needle', or as it seems to have been later corrupted, 'to thread the eye of the needle'. The 'eye' was the lamp niche, being illuminated in the illustration, which had been opened up to the passage beyond, and through which the young woman had to pass into the crypt, or needle.

About 1990, the distribution of apples was revived at the Cathedral. On Christmas Day in the late eighteenth century, *'the singing boys come into the church with large baskets full of red apples with a sprig of Rosemary stuck in each.'* [134] The apples symbolised life; the rosemary, death. They were presented to the congregation who, 'according to the quality of the lady or gentleman', rewarded the choirboys with 2d, 4d or 6d. In the nineteenth century the dean presented the choirboys with a sovereign at Christmas. This custom was revived at the same time as the apples, the choirboys each receiving a £1 coin from the dean.

With the ministri[135] of the Minster, who included the early wakemen, taking part, mystery plays were performed not only in the Minster itself but also in the streets and villages at Christmas, Epiphany and Easter. It is doubtful if the custom survived the Reformation, but the Ripon Sword Dance - a mummers' play - was a regular part of the Christmas festivities until 1914; revived after 1918 and again in the late 1930s. The present play - the usual version involving St. George - updates an 1880s play and does not seem to be a long tradition in the city. The Wakeman Mummers' Play was written by James Coulson in 1986 for the Ripon 1100 celebration. Accompanying the setting of the watch, it is presented during the August St. Wilfrid's Festival in the market place and closes with the distribution of specially baked, horn-shaped, wholemeal biscuits.

A tithe barn stood on Priest Lane until it was demolished in June 1926. To support the church, you would expect to pay a tithe (one tenth) of your labour and produce. But in Ripon, you would have also to pay five shillings a year to the dean and chapter for every milk cow you kept; and on your death, your next of kin would have to pay a 'mortuary' or heriot, usually your second-best beast or coat, to the church. In 1833 the Darnboroughs of Blossomgate, whose tenth child was due, had their cottage utensils sold at auction for two shillings and sevenpence halfpenny (about l3p) towards their tithe. Later they were reported as having decided to christen the new baby Tithe and send him to the dean and chapter as their Easter offering.[136]

The Wakeman Mummers.

The Ripon City Morris Dancers were formed in 1982 and dance the north-west Morris. They are firm favourites, appearing regularly both in the city and the surrounding area. Unusually, they wear fresh flowers around their hats.

Fun and games

The customary way to help the beggars and vagrants who regularly passed through the city in the nineteenth century, and make sure that the gift was not spent on alcohol, was to use Cocoa House tokens, which could be exchanged for a mug of hot cocoa and something to eat at the Cocoa House in Westgate, now Davill's Bakery.

In 1986 the city hosted Ripon 1100, a year celebrating 1100 years since the mythical King Alfred charter; a smaller festival has been held at Spring Bank holiday each year since. Two events from 1986 have continued with increasing popularity. On Boxing Day, a procession sets out from the Cathedral, led by the bishop, symbolically to follow the path taken by the founding monks of Fountains Abbey. Also, each New Year's Eve, after a short watch-night service, led by the city band, a torchlight procession of the order of 1,000 people makes its way from the Cathedral to the market place, where even more gather to hear the hornblower sound the final watch for the year, and to receive greetings from the mayor and a blessing from the dean.

Wife sales were not legal but certainly went on, and there was an acknowledged way of going about it. The bellman, or town crier, would announce that the lady was to be sold on a given market day. Although it did not happen in all instances, the husband would lead the lady, usually in a halter, round the market place and then put her up for auction. Often the purchaser had been pre-arranged. Afterwards, the parties would retire to a local hostelry where 'papers'

The Boxing Day walk - Ripon Cathedral to Fountains Abbey - follows the route of the founding monks.

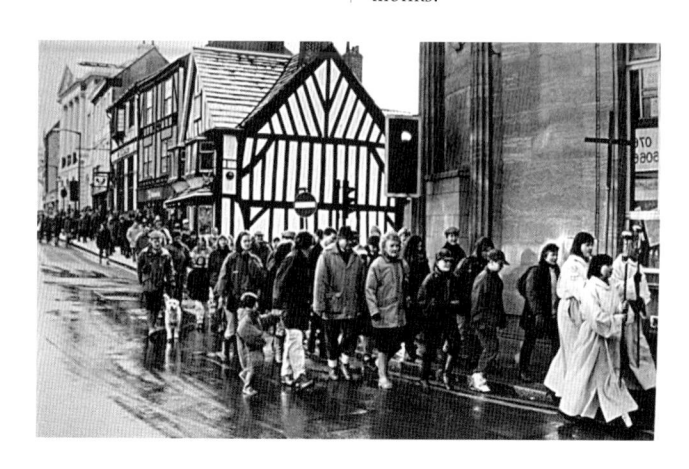

would be signed, over a stamp, and jollities would commence. Sometimes the new husband would literally step into the shoes of his predecessor. The last recorded wife sale in Ripon is thought to be that of Mrs. Dunn who told, in 1881, of having been sold to Dunn for twenty-five shillings. She had the documentation to prove it - very important to maintain her respectability.[137]

Possibly originally linked to the seven prebends or estates of the Minster, the select vestry formed the churchwardens of the parish between the dissolution of the chapter in 1547 and the re-establishment of the collegiate church in 1604, one member for each of the four wards of the town and one each for the three outlying chapelries: Bishop Monkton, Sawley and Bondgate. Perhaps another ancient link is suggested by the fact that the jailer and master of the house of correction carried white staffs in the procession for the start of the liberty quarter sessions.[138] Seemingly, when Bondgate was finally assimilated into the borough of Ripon in the late nineteenth century, the select vestry was increased to eight.[139] Normally the select vestry of churchwardens was elected at the annual vestry meeting of those householders liable to pay the poor rate and, with the overseers of the poor, the select vestry was responsible for the administration of the old Poor Law. All holders of public office were required to be members of the Established Church and, if there was doubt, the churchwardens would be called to testify. One set of the black staves carried by the city stave-bearers has large knobs on the end, quite fearsome weapons. Under the 1734 Bastardy Act, a child was entitled to have the mother's settlement and the mother a public whipping. In some parishes, persuasion would be applied to the putative father by the parish officers, backed up by the knobsticks, to assume his responsibilities and avoid a charge upon the rates - hence the expression 'knobstick wedding'.

Tops of select vestry staves at Ripon Cathedral.

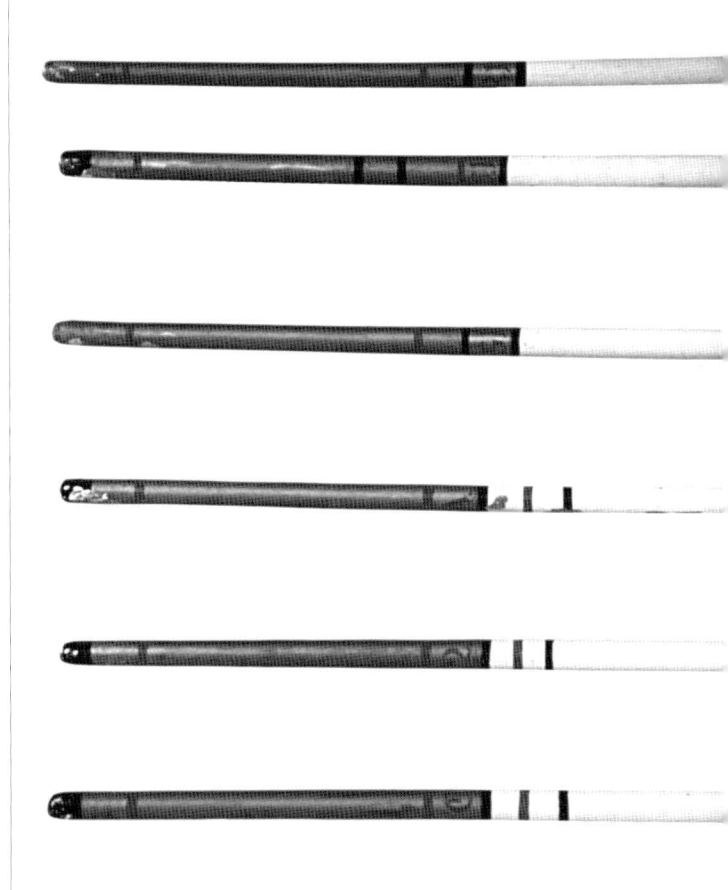

Fun and games

The creation of new select vestries appears to have stopped after the 1688 Revolution. Attempts to reform those that existed began about the same time 'to prevent the poor being cheated', and for some 200 years a dummy bill, 'A Bill to Reform Select Vestries', was introduced into the House of Lords. In an Act of 1818, known as the Sturges Bourne Act, parishes were authorised to establish a standing committee of between five and twenty persons, to be called the select vestry, and nearly 3,000 were established. They were to deal solely with poor relief and appoint an overseer of the poor. Because of their abuse of the poor rate, it is said, 'select vestry' became synonymous with robbery and corruption.[140]

The Minster was Ripon's parish church, but as a collegiate church it lost its municipal powers, firstly at the Reformation and then by the royal charter of 1604, which established the corporation. Because of its widespread area - some forty townships comprised the liberty - it was not possible for the ecclesiastical parish to operate as a civil parish, and for law and order, the townships were divided into twenty three constabularies.

After the demise of ecclesiastical control, the powers of a select vestry for the civil parish of Ripon had been subverted by a network of local worthies controlled by the Studley Estate, a number of whom sat as both members of the corporation and as justices of the peace. The effect of the Act of 1818 was to open up the 'scandalous' situation prevailing in Ripon - the matter went to law in 1822. Lawyers for the newly appointed select vestry claimed that:

'The borough justices [the aldermen] although no sessions of the peace are held in Ripon ... have always transacted the business relating to the poor of the borough, but there is no special or local act [of Parliament] relating to the poor, nor is there any select vestry established by usage or custom'.[141]

In 1889, the chancellor of the diocese ruled that, whilst not holding civil responsibilities, the select vestry at the Cathedral held their office 'by good custom'. Its members nowadays have a largely symbolic role, assisting with the seating of the congregation and attending the clergy, but formerly their duties included enforcing attendance at worship and taking action against dissidents. Until the system of pew-renting was suppressed in the mid-nineteenth century, the select vestry was involved in the allocation of seating in the choir, which, with its box pews and galleries, is estimated to have accommodated about a thousand worshippers. The select vestry may also have been responsible for, or served as, the 'dog whippers', removing dogs from the Minster, and for waking those who fell asleep during the long sermons - tasks for which, no doubt, their white staves would prove useful.

To cure the eyes and to heal bandy-legged children, the place to go was St. Wilfrid's Well on Skellbank. There is a reference to fields *'at Westgate end near St.Wilfrey Well'* in 1606. In addition to its curative properties, in the eighteenth century water was channelled from this well to High Mill for paper making.

St. Wilfrid's Well, Skellbank.

Fun and games

Served by Samuel Butler's touring company, which included the famous Edmund Kean amongst its actors, the old St. Wilfrid's Feast of the 20th August 1792 saw the first performance at Ripon's new Theatre Royal, although the company had performed in the town two years previously. George Hassell, recorder of the borough, is usually credited with the building of the 320 seat theatre in 1792, but he had died fourteen years earlier. The company tended to visit Ripon in the winter, seeking support for their performances from individuals and groups. After his father's death, Butler's son kept the group together into the 1830s. Under the heading 'Thorne's Theatre, Ripon', a playbill of 1839 announces performances of 'Hut of the Red Mountain' and 'All the World's a Stage' on Monday the 25th February, and on Wednesday the 27th the grand Scottish operatic drama 'Rob Roy', together with a new farce. Prices were: boxes 2s, pit 1s, gallery 6d. Where such performances would have been held is uncertain. Ripon's theatre had become a military riding school in 1826, and later a drill hall. It was destroyed by fire in 1918, having stood close to the junction of Park Street and Firby Lane. From 1851, Ripon Dramatic Society performed in the Public Rooms (i.e. the Edward Room), at the Victoria Opera House (later the Victoria Hall) until 1853. In 1857, in his journal, Charles Dodgson recorded twice attending concerts at the Public Rooms.

A playbill for Ripon Theatre 1798. Notice that Mr. Butler and Mr. W. Butler both appear.

However, in 1853, it was announced:

The members of the Ripon Amateur Dramatic Society have great pleasure in announcing to their many friends and public in general, the opening of this new elegant and commodious theatre which has been erected (at tremendous cost) from an architectural design by J.C.Bennet Esq., of Leeds, and which for magnitude effect and comfort, far surpasses anything before attempted in the City of Ripon or its immediate vicinity, and capable of accommodating several hundred persons. The interior has been fitted up with great care, and the arrangement of the boxes, pit and gallery, are such as cannot fail to give satisfaction.... Every precaution has been taken to render the theatre impervious to rain, (the cover being of waterproof material).

It is not easy to work out if this New Theatre Royal was a permanent structure, where it stood, and how much 'tongue-in-cheek' was used in its name. The reference to the waterproof cover suggests that it might have replaced some leaky marquee, or similar, which stood on the old Fair Field (Treasurer's Garth) where Westbourne Grove and Zion Chapel were later built. Possibly it stood nearer Westgate - more recently the fire station/car showroom site. On opening night, the society performed the drama 'William Tell', followed by a pantomime 'St. Wilfrid in the Olden Time'. [142]

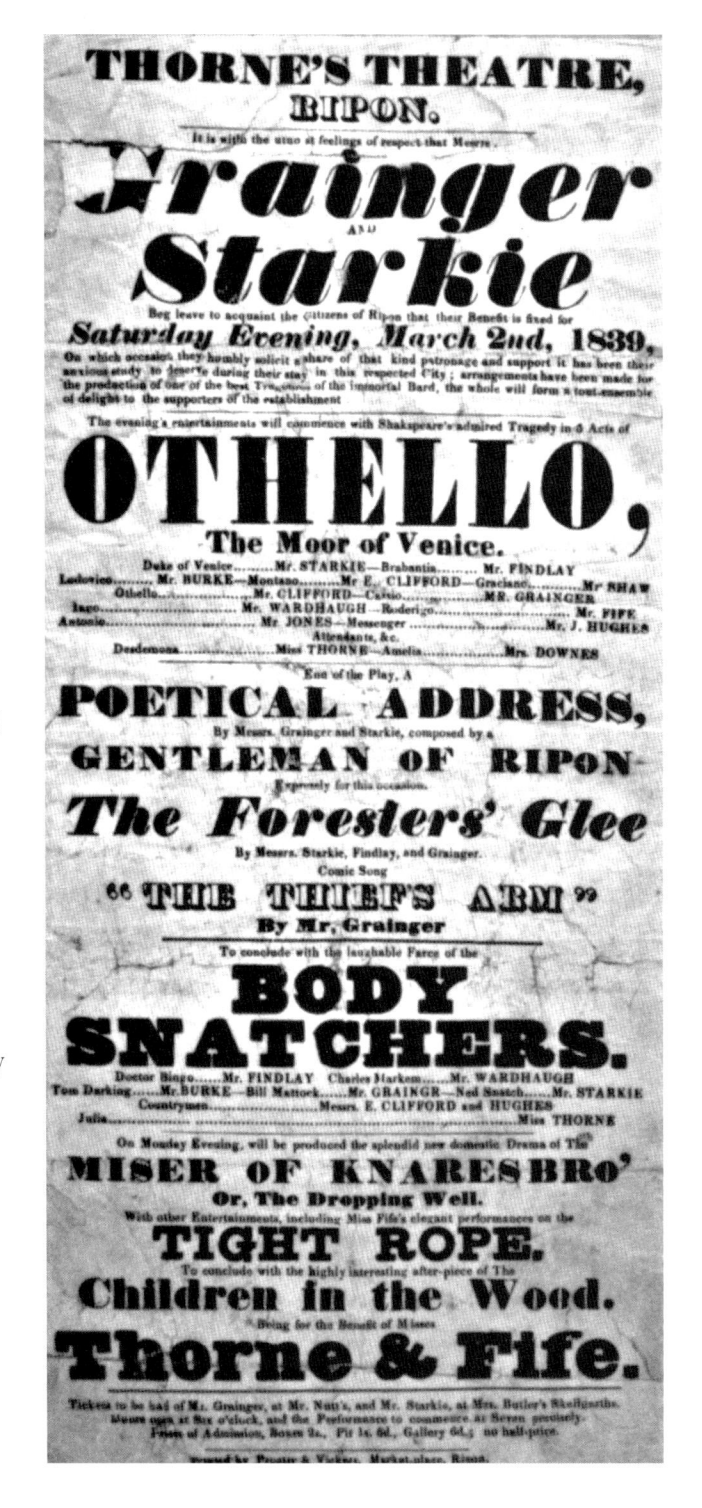

A playbill of the performance by Thorne's Theatre in Ripon on 2nd March 1839.

Fun and games

Another diversion lost with the enclosure of the commons was walking the maze. Known as the Maidens Bower, it had been re-cut in 1809 on the triangle of land bounded by Palace Road, Little Studley Road and Spring Bank. A similar maze, existed at Asenby, near Topcliffe. In 2001, the maze was reconstructed by the Rotary Club on Spa Park.

From 1801, Ripon society was able to meet for cards and balls in the assembly rooms, now the town hall.

In 1832, after the Tory owners had denied access to the assembly rooms (town hall) to their political opponents, public rooms were built which became the meeting place for all political parties. Rebuilt to seat 1,000 in 1885, it was known as the Victoria Hall, or Opera House, but after twenty years was up for sale. In 1909 it became a roller-skating rink, until it was converted to one of Ripon's three cinemas in 1917. A second cinema, the Palladium, operated in Kirkgate from 1916-82, and during the First World War a third cinema opened: the Spa, on the Spa Park site. In 1928, having run into difficulties, the corporation was given first option to buy the Opera House (Victoria Hall site), but the Wellington Film Co. took a twenty-year lease and re-opened it as a cinema. Ripon's first talkies were shown there in February 1930, although for the first performance the electricity supply failed. The Opera House continued showing films until 1967 when, unable to compete with television, it became a bingo and function room. In 1970, the council decided to purchase it but could not agree a price. Six years later it was gutted by fire. A scheme to convert it to a community centre came to nothing, and it is now Sigma Antiques at the junction of Water and Low Skellgate.

Originally built as a workshop for Croft and Blackburn, coach builders, in the nineteenth century, the Palladium was the longest of Ripon's cinemas to survive. It is now a nightclub.

A museum on Park Street had been established in 1883. Twenty years later its site became part of the Spa Gardens, and the artefacts were moved to the town hall until a city museum was begun in 1913 at Thorpe Prebend House. That museum survived until September 1956, two years later than the Wakeman's House Museum. Ripon Museum Trust was formed in 1981 to establish the Prison and Police Museum in St. Marysgate. In 1996, they opened a Poor Law Museum in part of the old workhouse and in 2001 the former magistrate's court.

The Church Institute had occupied a room in the town hall until the building was presented to the corporation and they were dispossessed when the room was required as the mayor's parlour. On land given by Miss Darnborough in 1899 they built themselves premises on the eastern side near the top of High Skellgate - the building with the steeply pitched gable. The Institute was short-lived and in 1917 the building was bought by the corporation for £100.

After several attempts to establish a proper lending library in the city, books were placed in the town hall by the West Riding County Council in 1928. Its success was such that, seven years later, a county library opened in Skellgarths. It moved to new premises in the Arcade shopping complex during 2001.

By 1813, Ripon had one of the most successful and best-supported cricket clubs in Yorkshire.[143] In 1892, the pavilion was at the eastern edge of the ground, but in 1902 a new pavilion opened on the opposite side. Having been given first option, the club purchased its field from Mr Clare Vyner for £1,200 in 1927.

Before the Mallorie Park Drive courts were built, tennis was played behind the Mechanics Institute on Finkle Street. In 1924, an application for Sunday tennis was refused. The tennis club sold its Mallorie Park ground to build a tennis centre on Palace Road, which opened in April 1996.

Bowling was and still is a popular pastime in Ripon, and there was a bowling club in the city in 1896. A new bowling club was formed in 1918 which played at the site of the old waterworks (now The Atrium, near North Bridge).

In December 1922, the city council agreed to extend the Spa Gardens bowling green and construct two all-weather hard tennis courts at the Spa, costing £225, which appears to have led to the formation of the Ripon Spa Gardens Bowling Club in 1923. The oldest member of the Spa Bowling Club, Mr Cliff Marshall, has stated he understood it occupied the site of the tennis courts. The Spa Park tennis courts date from May 1926.

The year 1906 saw plans for the creation of a golf club at Studley Park, using the northern gate-house as the club room, with the course on the northern side of the main driveway. Within two years the golf club at Palace Road was inaugurated. In January 1943, Studley Park was ploughed up as part of the war effort. Ripon City Golf Club extended their golf house in 1972, and their course from nine to eighteen holes in 1993.

AN ILLUSTRATED HISTORY OF RIPON

Fun and games

Ripon City Band on the Cathedral tower during the 1935 jubilee celebrations.

Ripon United Football Club were runners up in the Harrogate Whitworth cup in June 1907. They amalgamated with Ripon City FC in August 1919, but were threatened with closure in 1935 unless attendances improved. Possibly, to that end, they switched leagues from York, in which they had played for twelve years, back to Allertonshire. May 1958 was a memorable year, when they won the Ripon League senior charity cup and the reserves won the junior cup. The club continues to play at Mallorie Park. Ripon Rugby Club, which celebrated its centenary in the late 1980s, has two pitches and clubhouse facilities, also at Mallorie Park.

The earliest reference to a band is from 1852, when 'a band of music' preceded St. Wilfrid in the procession instead of the customary fife. This band appears to have been short-lived - in 1860 the mayor and corporation handed the instruments 'previously used by the City Band' to the newly formed volunteer band of the Ripon Rifles, on condition that they paid the £24 debt on them. Ten years later we read again: *'Volunteer band formed. The instruments belonging to the old City band, were handed over to the volunteer officers on condition that the band played once a week in the Market Place',* but by November 1898 new instruments costing £50 10s were purchased. The band seems to have continued a precarious existence - two Beckwith brothers ending up in court in 1906 after coming to blows following a general meeting to disband and sell the instruments, but it carried on with borrowed instruments. The year 1919 saw them moving into premises on High St. Agnesgate, when the city council agreed to their use of *'the first floor of the warehouse adjoining the City Museum as a rehearsal room at a nominal rent of £2 per annum'*.

In August 1944, the people watching the Wilfrid Procession were disappointed that the saint had already passed by before they were aware of his coming, as he 'proceeded silently and unannounced because no musical accompaniment could be found'. After the war things got underway again, and in November 1961 the mayor launched an appeal for £1,000 to pay for new uniforms for the Ripon City Silver Band. Four years later and now titled Ripon City Prize Band, a supporters' club was formed, converting a disused shop on the ground floor of their headquarters into a clubroom.

Ripon Choral Society was founded in 1954 by Elvet English, Harry Graham, Frank Orton and Jim Hall, who had begun by singing as a male voice group, the Ripon Musical Society, before introducing female voices and changing the name. It has a strong following in the city.

Dr (then Mr) C.H. Moody was appointed organist to the Cathedral in January 1902. Some three years later, at his instigation, Ripon Operatic Society was formed, At his insistence a professional coach and a full professional orchestra were thought essential, although not everyone was in agreement. Four performances of their first production, 'The Pirates of Penzance', took place in March 1905, including a Thursday matinee for the benefit of country patrons, but it was at the Friday gala night when everybody who was anybody arrived in full evening dress and stayed for the Opera Ball (tickets strictly limited) in the Edward Room. The year 1906 brought 'Iolanthe' in February and a lavish production of 'Merrie England' for the festival. The succeeding years produced 'The Mikado', 'The Yeoman of the Guard', 'The Gondoliers', 'Patience', 'Pinafore', 'Dorothy' and 'Les Cloches de Corneville', and in February 1914, 'Falka'.

Dr Moody's Amateur Operatic Society was revived in 1921, a little less exclusively, adding 'Tom Jones' in 1928 but generally repeating most of its previous shows, including 'Les Cloches de Corneville' in 1932. Then came a major difference of opinion within the society over artistic policy, and it was nine years before 'The Pirates of Penzance' re-appeared. George Jackson wrote in 1950: *'the history of the third phase of opera in Ripon is too recent to require a setting out in detail ... [but] we are grateful for a continuance of the operatic tradition. May its reign be long and its members enjoy all the success they deserve.'* The society continues to thrive.

Ripon Photographic Society celebrated its fiftieth anniversary in 1999, having been founded by Leon Smallwood and Geoff Watts. In 1948, Mr Smallwood had taken over Cox's photographic studio, established in 1860 in Kirkgate, where the society originally met.

Back to school

It has been suggested that both a grammar and a song school existed in Ripon as early as the tenth century. One can go back further and say that formal education can be traced to the seventh-century monastery where Wilfrid brought Eddius to teach chanting, and where St. Willibrord, bishop of Utrecht and apostle to the Frisians, was sent as a child to be educated. Today, visitors from Echternach come to Ripon in search of the school Willibrord attended.

Evidence suggests that the 1555 grammar school charter should be regarded as the re-foundation of the school, in response to a local petition. There was certainly a school at Ripon by 1348, when the sheriff of Yorkshire was ordered to bring Richard the Chamberlain, formerly master of the schoolhouse of Ripon, with 137 others to Court. From the fourteenth century, the schoolhouse is recorded 'in the old place at the corner of Agnesgate, just below the Minster', and reference has been made already to St. John's Hospital which, in the twelfth century, supported 'poor clerks keeping their schools at Ripon, four or five of whom were to have soup daily and beds at night'. St. John's was re-endowed in 1340, partly to support a chaplain and poor boys attending the grammar schools in Ripon. In 1468, the Minster chapter prohibited the establishment of any other school without their licence.

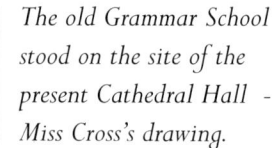

The old Grammar School stood on the site of the present Cathedral Hall - Miss Cross's drawing.

The Reformation broke the chapter's monopoly - indeed, under the Chantries Act, the grammar school closed in 1548. To regain the school, and a dubious income for at least one of the governors, a conspiracy developed to hide from the king's commissioners the fact that some school land was chantry and gild land, which risked confiscation. A quarrel flared between the governors and the schoolmaster, and in 1550 the truth came out. Five years later, the grammar school was endowed with the revenues of four of the dissolved chantry chapels.[144] Masters were taking boarders by 1729. In 1814 there were, in addition to the boarders, seventeen foundation scholars who were entitled to free education, but the school was struggling financially against competition from the new National schools.

In 1811, the Church of England had set up its National Society for Promoting the Education of the Poor, using a system developed by Dr Andrew Bell, an Anglican clergyman, in which a master conducted the school in a single large room with the cleverer boys assisting with the instruction. The basis of the system was reward and punishment, seen as moral training: the best boy in the group would earn a halfpenny, but disobedience could result in the culprit being made to wear a dunce's cap or receiving a public washing. The floggings of the public schools were not part of the National school system.[145]

There is a reference to 'Mr Pickersgill's School' at Bishopton Grove in 1842, which Thomas Darnborough, mayor, born in 1792, had attended. One former pupil wrote that in 1819, at the age of eight, in 'black and hopeless misery' he was 'abandoned at a school near Ripon' for four years.[146] That was Henry George Liddell, whose daughter Alice was later to be immortalised in 'Alice in Wonderland'.

Liddell became dean of Christ Church, Oxford, where Charles Dodgson (Lewis Carroll) was a mathematics tutor. Incidentally, Charles Dodgson wrote that, on one occasion, he took his youngest brother Edwin to Mr Jefferson's school at North Stainley. This school had originated in Sharow.

The other Bishopton school, variously known as Charnock Academy and Bishopton Close Academy, was built in 1826 by Miss Lawrence of Studley for Rev. Jas Charnock. In 1873, the headmaster of Bishopton Close School, as it was then known, William Fowler Stephenson, died suddenly, aged forty-five. The marquis of Ripon, chairman of the grammar school governors, negotiated the site for the grammar school, which transferred there in 1874. The Cathedral hall now stands on the site of the old grammar school.[147]

During the early 1870s, two new sites were being considered for the grammar school: at the Park Street/Firby Lane junction (the Drill Field); and at the Clotherholme Road junction with Studley Road. Negotiations for the first of these sites were well advanced. William Burges, the architect of Studley and Newby churches, had drawn up plans, and significant compensation had to be paid when the Bishopton Close site was adopted.

In 1919, Mr CS Bland retired after twenty-four years as head of the grammar school. During his time, a laboratory block, sanatorium and swimming pool had been provided, but it was noted that numbers, which had risen from 68 to 110, would have been higher had it not been for competition from Jepson's Hospital, which educated forty boys up to fourteen years for £4 a year against £15 at the grammar school.

Back to school

Jepson's Hospital - the 'bluecoat' school, from the blue and yellow uniforms - operated in Water Skellgate from 1672 until 1927, when the head teacher and the remaining scholars transferred to the grammar school. Little is known of the founder himself, Zacarias Jepson. He was born in Ripon and moved to York where he practised as an apothecary, becoming a freeman aged twenty-nine. He married Isobel Man of Clifton in 1653 and died, aged forty-nine, in 1672. He is buried in Ripon Cathedral graveyard. He left almost everything for the foundation of a hospital (boarding) school for twenty orphan boys or poor freemen's sons, born in Ripon, who were to be at least seven years old when admitted and could stay until they were fifteen and a half. Those suitable were to attend Oxford or Cambridge universities, which seven did over its lifetime. Numbers had to be adjusted because the original endowment did not match Jepson's expectations, but with an income of £176 7s 3d in 1828 to support ten foundation scholars, the school was reckoned to be in a good financial position. Whilst the inspector's reports on the non-classical schools do not include much criticism of the schoolmasters, it was noted that the master of Jepson's should be more attentive, and should teach the boys arithmetic.[148] The school was rebuilt in 1878, but a succession of financial difficulties towards the end of the nineteenth century was not helped by considerable criticism from the Charity Commissioners. In 1895, in addition to the foundation boys, the school was extended to take fifty boys at £2 2s each a year. After the school closed in 1927 the site was bought by T & R Williamson, varnish manufacturers, to extend their factory, and the school building became the City Club.[149]

Jepson's staff and pupils about 1915.

Alma House as Skellfield School.

Serving as Ripon Girls' High School from 1908 to 1962 when it was amalgamated into Ripon Teacher Training College In 2001 the building became part of Leeds Metropolitan University.

The High School, Ripon, opened in 1877 in St. Wilfrid's Terrace. Within a year it had moved to Fountains Terrace, and almost immediately afterwards transferred to Alma House, changing its name to the High School, Skellfield, Ripon, where it stayed until 1927. 'High School' was dropped from the title in the early 1880s. The school ran into debt and the head, Miss Roser, departed, taking most of the pupils with her. However, it survived and built up a good reputation. In 1927 it transferred to Baldersby Park, closing in the 1950s.[150] The author Naomi Jacob was a day pupil.

On land bought from Ripon Training College, amidst considerable local opposition, a scheme for a secondary school for girls went ahead. It opened in January 1908 with Miss Minnie Davie as head, three teachers and twelve scholars, and quickly changed its name to Ripon Girls' High School. Miss Davie resigned in June 1911 against 'not a little prejudice' to any higher education for girls. Her successor survived five years and in 1916 Miss M.W. Johnson was appointed. She served until 1948, to be succeeded by Miss J.M. Cullingworth. By 1920 there were 140 pupils, but the buildings had only been designed for eighty and as an evening institute. In 1962, with 260 girls on roll, it was decided to amalgamate with the boys' grammar school.

In the late fifteenth and early sixteenth centuries, plans were advanced to establish a 'university of the north', to be sited at Ripon, to try to enhance the teaching of religion in an area where loyalty to the old faith still held support. But Ripon's aspirations were thwarted and the honour went to Durham. An attempt in 1963-4 to persuade the government to site one of the new universities in Ripon also failed.

Back to school

An early view of the Ripon College for Training Elementary Schoolmistresses.

For twenty years, from 1898, Ripon did become a centre of theological learning with the establishment of Ripon Clergy College at the end of Princess Road, near the Clock Tower. One of the students was Geoffrey Studdert Kennedy, better known as 'Woodbine Willie', the most famous army chaplain of the First World War. As 'Ripon Hall', the college moved to Oxford in 1919.

Using premises in Monkgate, York, vacated by the men's college, in 1846 a college was founded for training schoolmistresses to work in the National schools. Following strong criticism by government inspectors, this transferred to Ripon in 1862, accommodating sixty students in new buildings on what became College Road for a two-year training course.[151] The buildings were extended in 1899 when there were about a hundred students. In 1975 it became the College of Ripon and York St. John, amalgamating with the men's college at York, and more recently became a university college offering other degree courses to some 2,000 students, adopting the name 'Ripon and York'. Its transfer back to York was announced in 1999, and the Ripon campus closed in 2001.

Previously a boys' boarding school, the Ripon Industrial Home for Girls stood opposite Bondgate Hall. In 1862, a number of 'benevolent ladies' raised £500 to buy and develop it as a residence for forty girls *'especially those who are motherless ...'* A moving account of her life in the home was written by Alice Collier.[152] The buildings were demolished in 1946.

The Ripon Industrial Home for Girls, Bondgate, prior to 1927.

There were fifteen National schools in Ripon by 1833, twelve of them opening in the 1820s: some were very small, most were fee paying. By 1722, St. John's Hospital was being used as a school. In 1812 it proudly adopted the National Society's 'Dr Bell's System' of mutual instruction, transferring in 1853 to a new building in Priest Lane as the Cathedral Boys' School. Forty years later, the dean gave his field near the school, on which Ripon House now stands, as a recreation ground for the children. The school closed in 1962. Pupils transferred either to the new Moorside School or Cathedral Primary School, which traces its history back to a National school for girls in the early nineteenth century. Construction of new buildings for the Cathedral Primary School on a site between Priest Lane and Cathedral Close began in 2001.

Architect's drawing for the Cathedral Boys' National School on Priest Lane, with the Methodist Chapel adjacent, both now demolished.

Holy Trinity School was built in 1836 on Trinity Lane, extended in 1888 and later. A new building for juniors was added on Church Lane in the 1970s. The Wesleyans also ran a school, for which 1870 is given for laying the foundation stone, but a Wesleyan National school existed in 1859.[153] In 1863, St. Wilfrid's Roman Catholic School opened for eighty mixed infants on Coltsgate Hill, transferring to Church Lane in August 1974.

Greystone Primary School opened on Quarry Moor Lane in November 1974.

Back to school

A class photograph from Ripon Council School, Coltsgate Hill, formerly the Wesleyan School.

In 1930, education in Ripon was re-structured. The closure of Coltsgate Hill Elementary School, condemned for some time, was announced in 1934; village children were to be given bicycles, or bussed into Ripon, either to the grammar school, the girls' high school or to a new non-selective senior school to be built to take 720 eleven to fourteen year olds. Ripon Modern School, the first school of its type to be built by the county council, opened in August 1939 with 480 pupils, becoming Ripon County Secondary School in the 1950s and Ripon City School in January 1982. It was granted technology college status in 1999, confusingly also adopting the name Ripon College.

Coltsgate Hill School buildings were brought back into use as the evacuation control centre for the 1,800 evacuees expected at the start of Second World War. In the end only 650 children and eighty mothers arrived to be billeted in the city.

The year 1946 saw the West Riding Education Committee suggest a 'multilateral' school for Ripon. Two years later it proposed closing the boys' grammar and girls' high schools and converting the Modern School into a mixed multilateral school. The protest was nothing to the uproar from the sporting fraternity in October 1950 at the proposal to build a new secondary school on the football ground in Mallorie Park Drive. In 1969 a middle school system was rejected.

Under instruction from the Labour government to introduce comprehensive education, in 1976 the North Yorkshire Education Committee eventually approved a single split-site school for eleven to eighteen year olds - 1,730 pupils in total, including 230 in the sixth form. After public consultation, the county council backed an alternative two-school scheme. This was referred back by the Minister of Education, who directed the council to prepare for a single comprehensive school in Ripon. The council took legal advice and it was ruled that the minister had exceeded her powers, but this was overturned by the High Court. Before an appeal could be heard, there was a general election and the new Conservative government withdrew the compunction to comprehensive education.

So fifty years after the initial first proposals to remove selection by academic ability from Ripon's educational system and perhaps reduce the proportion of pupils who leave Ripon each day for their secondary education, the debate on the advantages and disadvantages of selective education for the city continues. A referendum in 1999 to abolish Ripon's selective system was defeated and an appeal against an allegedly 'flawed' system was rejected by the Secretary of State.

In March 1960, the dean and chapter announced the purchase of St. Olave's Preparatory School, Whitecliffe Lane, - part of the old racecourse site, as a Cathedral choir school, funded largely by the sale of books from the Cathedral library, including two volumes printed by Caxton. In 2005 it applied to extend its facilities significantly.

Dr Barnardo's Bishop's Palace School for Girls opened in 1940, becoming ten years later Spring Hill School, a residential special school. Barnardo's also opened children's homes at Red House and West Mount, since closed.

One of the schools I am most often asked about is Westholme Girls' School and Kindergarten, whose principals were Miss Aslin and Miss Greenwood in the 1920s. Mrs. Aslin is recorded at Westholme in 1903 (the shift from the courtesy title 'Mrs' is perhaps a reflection of the changes brought about by the First World War). The school offered scripture, English, mathematics, literature, French, Latin, nature study, freehand and model drawing, class singing, harmony, theory of music and needlework. Particular emphasis was placed on music and 'physical culture'. Extras included pianoforte, solo singing, painting, gymnasium and elocution. The prospectus emphasised the liberal and varied diet, and that each pupil had a separate bed. For boarders under twelve, the fee was ten guineas per term (£10.50); for day pupils it was one and a half guineas per term (£1 57.5), with laundry, pew rent, stationery and books 'according to outlay'. Mr and Mrs Mylchreest were the principals when the school closed in the 1960s.

The former Westholme School, Park Street.

Heroes and villains

Frederick John 'Prosperity' Robinson, first Viscount Goderich and first Earl of Ripon. Colonial Secretary, Chancellor of the Exchequer and Prime Minister (1827). 'The most timid and fearful individual to hold high office in British affairs - always on the run whenever a serious difficulty appeared in his path'.

Mention has already been made of many people associated with Ripon's past. From the Anglo-Saxon period these include international religious figures such as Cuthbert, Wilfrid, Willibrord and Ceolfrid; and in the medieval period, archbishops of York such as Roger pont l'Evêque, Geoffrey Plantagenet, Walter de Gray, Thurstan, Corbridge and Melton. John of Ripon was lord abbot of Fountains from 1414 to 1435.

The earls of Northumberland and Westmorland touched Ripon's history, as did various royals - both in and out of favour - and Oliver Cromwell. Doubtful characters such as Drunken Barnaby and Eugene Aram appear; as do famous architects James Wyatt, Nicholas Hawksmoor, William Chambers, William Burges and Gilbert Scott.

The political Aislabies, John and William, were followed a century later at Studley Royal by George Frederick Samuel Robinson, marquis of Ripon, viceroy of India, who had been born at 10 Downing Street during his father's premiership.[154] Following the demise of power of the archbishops of York after the Reformation, 'Studley' controlled Ripon for over 200 years. In more recent times Neil Balfour, member of the European Parliament, and Paul Sykes, multi-millionaire developer, have occupied Studley Royal. Famous diarists Daniel Defoe, Celia Fiennes and Lord Torrington recorded their impressions of Ripon, as did John Leland for Henry VIII. Ripon's seventeenth-century benefactor Zacarias Jepson continues to enhance the lives of Ripon's young people with educational grants.

Aged fourteen, John Elliott circumnavigated the world with Captain Cook in the Resolution. He built Holmefield House in 1797. His inscription in Ripon Cathedral reads:

'In memory of the late John Elliott, Esq., of Elliott House, near Ripon, Commander R.N., having entered the service of his country early in life, he circumnavigated the globe as a midshipman in the "Resolution", under the command of the celebrated captain Cook; he subsequently served as lieutenant of the "Ajax" of 74 guns, and was present in Lord Rodney's glorious action of the 12th of April 1792, in which he was severely wounded. He resided at Elliott House many years, greatly respected for his strict integrity and uprightness in all the relations of life. He was born January 11th 1759, and died September 17th 1834.'

Sir William Chambers was a member of a Scottish family, some of whom settled in Ripon, others in Gothenberg, Sweden, where William was christened in February 1725. For his education he was sent to Ripon, under the care of his uncle Dr William Chambers, a surgeon, who lived in Market Place. After Chambers left Ripon Grammar School, he joined the Swedish East India Company, visiting Europe, especially France, and making three visits to China. During these years he studied modern languages, mathematics and architecture, gaining a reputation as a student of Chinese architecture and gardens. He was appointed as architect to the Dowager Princess Augusta and architecture tutor to her son, later George III. He was subsequently appointed architect to the king and Controller of Works. He was instrumental in developing the fashion for Chinoiserie, especially through his work on projects such as the Chinese Pagoda at Kew Gardens. He also designed Somerset House and the Coronation Coach, and was instrumental in founding the Royal Academy in 1768. His ingenuity in the design of staircases was recognised in the academy lectures by Sir John Soane and influenced the work of Robert Adam.[155]

Heroes and villains

An eighteenth-century murderer of some notoriety, Eugene Aram, was born at Ramsgill, Nidderdale, in 1704. His father, Peter, was gardener at Ripley Castle and Newby Hall. Whilst the family lived in Bondgate, between the ages of five or six until he was thirteen, Eugene attended school in Ripon where, he wrote, he *'was made capable of reading the Testament, which was all I ever was taught'*. Some say this school may have been the grammar school ; others that it was St. John's, Bondgate. If the latter is the case, the use of St. John's as a school before 1722 may have contributed to the discontinuance of the annual service after that year. Eugene Aram became a schoolmaster in Knaresborough, and in February 1745 was implicated in the murder of Daniel Clark, a young shoemaker, who had disappeared after obtaining a large number of goods on credit. Not long after Clark's disappearance, Aram paid off his own debts and left Knaresborough. Thirteen years later a skeleton, said to be Clark's, was found in St. Robert's Cave, Knaresborough. Aram was arrested at Kings Lynn, where he was teaching at the grammar school.[156] He was tried at York assizes on the 3rd August 1759, and despite defending himself in an impressive and scholarly manner, was found guilty. He was hanged on the 6th August, his body to be gibbeted at Knaresborough.[157] His story has been linked to Lewis Carroll's 'The Walrus and the Carpenter' from the metrical pattern of Thomas Hood's poem 'The Dream of Eugene Aram', popular at the time.

For sixteen years, Charles Dodgson (Lewis Carroll) was associated with Ripon, through his father who was a residentiary canon at the Cathedral from 1852. On one of his visits, in 1858, Carroll stayed at the Unicorn. In 'The Hunting of the Snark' one of the major characters is the Boots; another is the bellman. Letters, poems and mathematical treatises written in Ripon by Dodgson survive. 'Through the Looking-Glass' was 'added to' here. Henry Liddell, the father of Carroll's 'real-life Alice', attended school at Bishopton Grove.

Charles Dodgson (Lewis Carroll). An early photograph, thought to have been one of two taken in Ripon in 1855.

Facing page: Wilfred Owen's literary hideaway - Borrage Lane.

Memorial tablet to Naomi Jacob, Sirmione, Italy.

Another important literary link is with the poet Wilfred Owen, who wrote some of his most poignant works such as 'Futility', 'Arms and the Boy' and 'The Send Off', in rented rooms in Borrage Lane, whilst stationed at Ripon for three months during the First World War.

Naomi Jacob, a famous novelist in the first half of the twentieth century, was born in Ripon in 1884. She died at Sirmione, Italy, aged eighty. A number of her 'Me' books include autobiographical accounts of Ripon. I tend to think of this as her 'ode to the sausage':

'Another thing brings back those nursery teas, festival days like birthdays, and so forth, when we were allowed to have sausages. Not, let me hasten to say, those poor pale imitation sausages which are now offered to the public, but - Appleton's Sausages. Anyone who has lived in Ripon will remember what they were like. Poems in skins! Short, thick, of a beautiful pale pink colour with skins so thin and tender that before frying you didn't stab at them with a fork, you stuck them gently with a fine darning needle. Cooked slowly - for I have a profound contempt for those people who imagine that sausages can be cooked in five minutes - turned and encouraged, gently almost tenderly, to burst. What a delicious aroma filled the kitchen! How charmingly they frizzled, spat, and popped! On the dish they lay in symmetrical beauty - four large and two smaller sausages. How you "spun out" the eating of them, savouring the delicate flavour, masticating slowly so as not to lose the least fraction of the joy of eating - Appleton's sausages.'

She goes on, in similar vein, to describe Appleton's pork pies:

'The same shop made pies too. They were pies! Small, at, I think, 2d each, larger at 6d, 1s and larger sizes "to order". The paste was beautiful, the top shining through the application of white of egg. The inside was no "mound of mystery", it was real pork, tender and well flavoured, and the jelly, which surrounded the meat was, as my nurse used to say, "Good enough ter put life intiv a dying man, choose how!"[158]

Heroes and villains

The Reverend Sabine Baring-Gould who wrote 'Onward Christian Soldiers' was ordained at Ripon as was The Reverend Nicholls (husband of Charlotte Brontë), and Charlotte Brontë herself visited Norton Conyers in 1839, the house reputedly contributing one of the most important ingredients in Jane Eyre - the Graham family legend of a mad woman confined to the attic. Other literary links include novelist Barbara Taylor Bradford, who visits friends in Ripon and whose works have references to the area; Florence Bone lived in Spring Bank, Ripon, for a while; and Dorothy Una Ratciffe, author and poet, married at Ripon Registry Office in December 1932.

Elizabeth Garnett, born at Otley in 1839, after her husband's death, threw herself into missionary work amongst the navvies, especially those building the reservoirs on Dallowgill Moors. From a room

The pyramid gravestone of Charles Piazzi Smyth can be found in Sharow churchyard.

at the Residence, one issue of her 'Quarterly Letter to Navvies' ran to 155,000 copies. Remarkable amongst the remarkable women of her age, she was a profound influence on the social history of her time, but is afforded little recognition.[159]

In February 1900, Professor Charles Piazzi Smyth, astronomer royal for Scotland and Regius Professor of Practical Astronomy at the University of Edinburgh, eminent Egyptologist and famous pioneer photographer, died at Clova, Clotherholme Road, where he had installed his great solar spectrograph. The story is told that he contracted with a York firm to build him a camera, to be buried with him, substantial enough for him to photograph the Day of Judgement. He was buried in Sharow churchyard under a pyramid-shaped tombstone next to his wife, but without the camera.[160]

In the year 2000, Colonel Rookes Evelyn Bell Crompton was honoured in London, with the erection of a plaque on the site of Crompton's Kensington Court Lighting Company, for his pioneering work with electricity in the nineteenth century. He was born in 1845 at Sion Hill, Kirby Wiske, the son of Joshua Crompton, who was elected Liberal MP in Ripon's tumultuous elections of 1832. In 1852, Evelyn Crompton went to Miss Jefferson's school at Sharow, where his schoolmates included Edwin Dodgson, younger brother of 'Lewis Carroll'. After time in Gibraltar, in 1856 the family returned to England and moved to Azerley. After leaving Harrow School in 1864, Crompton lived in Paris for six months before joining the Rifle Brigade. He left the army in 1875, and worked on the water supply and drainage systems at Azerley, where he installed an up-to-date sewage system. He became a partner in a firm in Chelmsford, and also a partner in an iron works in Derbyshire,

before founding Crompton and Co, the first major British manufacturer of electricity generators, producing the generating equipment for Kensington power station and also some of the first domestic electric cookers. He took portable generators to the Henley Regatta and Alexandra Palace, and thrilled the public with spectacular electric demonstrations. Crompton's street lighting installations included those for King's Cross Station and the Law Courts. Abroad, his ambitious lighting system for the Vienna Opera House covered a wider area than had ever been attempted and people flocked to see Vienna's first electric street lamps. In the Boer War, he used his arclamp design to develop a full military searchlight, and during the First World War he advised on the design and production of the military tank. Crompton was awarded the Faraday Medal in 1926 for conspicuous service to the advancement of electrical science.

He was also a founder member of the Royal Automobile Club. He married heiress Elizabeth Clarke, daughter of George Clark of West Tanfield, in 1871. The couple moved back to the Azerley Estate in 1939, where Elizabeth died that year. Colonel Crompton died, aged ninety-four, in 1940 at Azerley.[161]

Bruce Oldfield, international fashion designer, whilst in the care of Dr Barnardos, was a pupil of Ripon Grammar School, as in the nineteenth century was Bishop William Stubbs, subsequently Regius Professor of History at Oxford, whose emphasis on the use of original documentary sources revolutionised the teaching of history. As a schoolboy, he had been given access to Ripon Cathedral library, the first major historian to examine it.

Heroes and villains

Bishop Charles Longley. After Ripon he became bishop of Durham, then archbishop of York and then archbishop of Canterbury, calling the first Lambeth Conference.

In 1836 the first bishop of Ripon, Charles Longley, went on to become bishop of Durham, archbishop of York and archbishop of Canterbury, calling the first Lambeth Conference. Bishop Boyd Carpenter, known as the silver-tongued preacher, had served as chaplain to Queen Victoria and became a personal friend, and after his appointment to Ripon remained in regular correspondence with her. He was called to administer the last rites and to assist at her funeral. Bishop John Moorman was senior Anglican observer for the archbishop of Canterbury at the second Vatican Council in 1966, an eminent theologian and author of 'A History of the Franciscan Order'.

A list such as this inevitably misses out many, but hopefully gives a flavour of those who have walked Ripon's paths and have influenced, or been influenced, by their time in this ancient place.

AN ILLUSTRATED HISTORY OF RIPON

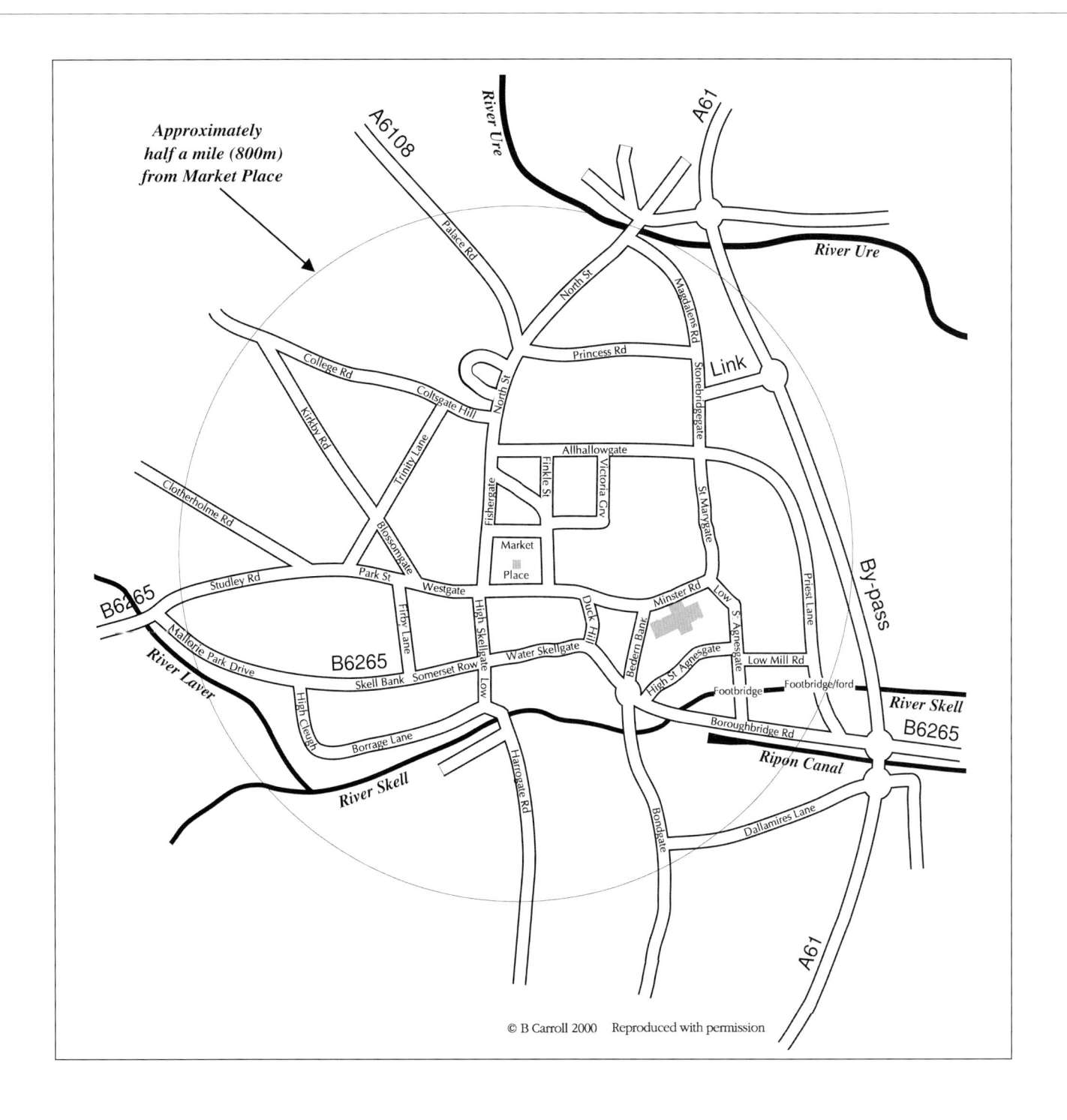

AN ILLUSTRATED HISTORY OF RIPON

Modern times

In 1836, Ripon Minster became Ripon Cathedral, and on the 17th November Revd. Charles Thomas Longley, first bishop of the new diocese of Ripon, arrived in the town and was formally introduced to his clergy, the mayor and corporation, and the principal inhabitants of the new city.[162]

The following year, Ripon's city status was formalised with its own bench of magistrates, recorder, clerk and coroner.[163]

However, in the Attorney General's opinion the corporation had no power to pay the salary of a recorder as the city did not have a separate quarter sessions - that belonged to the liberty - so the recorder's salary was refunded and the office abolished.[164] Local government reorganisation in 1974 would have seen the end of the coveted 'city' title, as Ripon became part of the Harrogate District, its local administration reduced to that of a parish council, but pride was restored to some extent when honorary city status was conferred under a charter granted by Elizabeth II on the 1st April 1975.

This chapter continues with a look at Ripon's local services. The dispensary was founded in Kirkgate in 1791, moving to the eastern end of High St. Agnesgate before settling on Firby Lane in 1850. The cottage hospital was added in 1888, and extended two years later; the separate nurses' home of 1903 now forms part of the hospital, linked by an elevated walkway. Because of the shortage of bricks, wooden buildings were used for the outpatients department, opened in 1948 on the opposite side of Firby Lane, but the closure of some departments towards the end of the century allowed the transfer of outpatient services to the main building, and the demolition of the wooden buildings provided additional car parking.

Changes in the funding of the Health Service have raised doubts over the future of the hospital, but as cottage hospitals seem again to be in favour, perhaps a future is more assured. In 2005 plans were announced for extensions to the building.

An isolation hospital, to accommodate fourteen paupers, opened in the workhouse grounds in 1878. It later became a geriatric hospital, St. Wilfrid's, closing in the re-organisations of the 1980s. A smallpox hospital for eight patients was built at Lark Hill, the highest point in the city, where the old waterworks had stood. From 1902 it served as a sanatorium for tuberculosis sufferers, and after that as a health resort for the poorest children in the city; it is long-since closed.[165]

The house of correction, St. Marygate, operated from 1684 until 1816 when the prison adjacent was added and the original building became the residence of the governor. From the 1820s, till it was removed in the 1860s, hard labour meant the tread wheel.
(Angus Rands)

112

To care for the poor, when the archbishop of York visited Ripon in 1684 he ordered the setting up of a workhouse and house of correction. The rule then was *'to whip and punish the wandering beggar'* - indeed, until 1713 beggars or wandering vagabonds were to be *'Grievouslye whipped and burnte through the gristle of the right eare'* with a hot iron an inch (25mm) wide, unless some honest householder owning land worth twenty shillings, or goods worth £5, agreed to take him into his service. Convicted again, the vagabond faced hanging.[166] Outdoor relief, the dole, was available to the poor of the parish: in desperation they could have indoor relief in the poor (or work) house. In 1776, the 'Old Hall' on Allhallowgate was conveyed by William Aislabie as the poorhouse, and that was where Ripon paupers went for relief. When the poor law changed in 1832 and outdoor relief was withdrawn from all but the sick, orphans and the aged, it took twenty years before the thirty-two local townships combined to form the Ripon Union.

In 1854 the new union workhouse, 'an almshouse-like building of comfortable human scale',[167] opened with accommodation for 120 paupers in separate male and female blocks. The buildings were enlarged, and in 1876 a vagrants block was added. The first master, George Greenwood, served until 1890. Better diets increased the cost of food by twenty-five per cent in 1901, and the board of guardians agreed in principle to the boarding out of children, but it did not happen. Ten years later the guardians were heavily criticised for keeping children in the workhouse and because the number of casual inmates was too high.

Above: On the site of an earlier Poorhouse, Ripon Workhouse operated here from 1854 - 1929. The building, now known as Sharow View, houses a range of County Council and voluntary services as well as the Ripon Poor Law Museum.

Modern times

Christmas dinner at Ripon Workhouse.

Originally tramps, those in search of a job, were distinguished from vagrants, the idle poor, but later the distinction faded. So that the vagrants could be properly housed for work within the institution, they were separated from the paupers. A new wood-chopping shed was added in 1903 and a day room followed in 1927. The name 'workhouse' changed to 'poor law institution' in 1913, but things seem to have gone on much as before. Canon Levick, the Roman Catholic priest, complained in 1927 that, because of the strict segregation, he had to say mass twice: once for the paupers, once for the vagrants. He was reprimanded by his fellow guardians for his criticisms of the casual wards. In the same year, vagrancy was almost double the previous years, and amongst the vagrants the guardians were 'distressed to find so many males ... who have fought and been maimed in the great War, and the country, after all the promises made on its behalf, has failed to stand by them'.[168]

Workhouses became obsolete following the introduction of old-age pensions and 'lunatic asylums', like Menston and Whixley. Ripon Workhouse closed in 1929, the vagrants cell-block last being used for that purpose in 1951. The buildings became an old people's home until June 1974 when the residents were transferred to new premises at Ripon House. The vagrants cell block is now a Poor Law museum.

Until the end of the nineteenth century, punishment by the payment of fines was rare. It was the responsibility of magistrates to deter others by making an example of the culprit. If that failed, the 'morbid member' faced transportation or execution. Most of those convicted at Ripon's quarter sessions, up to the 1830s, were *whipped at the market cross till their backs be bloody*. Towards the end of the eighteenth century, the refinement of being fastened to the back of a cart and 'whipped with a cat of nine tails' around the market place at two o'clock on market day had developed. In 1800, George Willis, bellman, was paid five shillings for each whipping.

Up to the 1834 Reform Act, the liberty and the township were policed by parish constables, whose wages were sanctioned through the magistrates at the quarter sessions. With new powers, and having been ejected from the town hall, from 1836-52 the council leased the building at the junction of Duck Hill and Kirkgate as their town house and police station, set up a watch committee and, in addition to the two nightwatchmen, appointed two police officers, the former parish constables. In 1838 they built their own lock-up, the entrance to which can be seen at the foot of the steps on Duck Hill.

Duck Hill steps and old lock up.

Modern times

The magistrates courthouse (1830) stands on the site of the medieval archbishops' palace. The building, extended at the rear in 1981, replaced one of 1770, on the same site.[169] It closed as a court and was acquired as offices by the dean and chapter in 2000, when the 1830 courthouse was leased to the Museum Trust.

In the early 1850s, there were many grumbles about the inefficiency of the police force and the senior policeman, Sweeting, was sacked. He sued, successfully, for payment of salary, but failed to be re-instated. Throughout the country, pressure was building for policing to be better organised, and in 1856 every county was required to establish a police force. The police inspectorate was pushing Ripon to join the West Riding Constabulary, but in Yorkshire there was enormous opposition to moving to a new system. Ripon Council kept the borough out of the West Riding Constabulary, but the surrounding liberty was absorbed into the Claro local government division. It is not clear from where the West Riding Constabulary operated in Ripon, although in 1856 they tried unsuccessfully to take over the old courthouse, where the liberty police had used the cells as lock-ups. In November 1856 the watch committee recommended that the city council appoint 'fit men' - a superintendent and five constables - costing £270 a year, but until 1875 the council continued with their two policemen and two nightwatchmen.[170]

It is perhaps of interest to note that a list of special constables, appointed in January 1868, includes Edwin Dodgson, the youngest brother of Charles Dodgson (Lewis Carroll). In 1862, the council took over a house in High Skellgate as the police office, but in 1875, when Thomas Metcalfe was appointed chief police officer, the police office moved from High Skellgate to 5 Kirkgate. At the same time the council did away with the nightwatchmen and appointed two constables instead.

Having been arrested for drunkenness in March 1877, and thrown into the Duck Hill lock-up, Richard Seaburgh, boilermaker, set his bedding alight and suffocated. After this tragedy the city council bought 5 Kirkgate as their police station and collector's office, at a cost of £1,847, which included alterations to provide four cells on the first floor - the barred windows of which can be seen from Duck Hill - linked to the ground floor of the police station on Kirkgate. Part of the building housed the fire engine.

Before the Prison Commission (now the Home Office) was set up, local prisons were the responsibility of the justices. During 1874 the prison on St. Marygate housed eleven males and two females. Within four years, with Scarborough and Beverley, it had been closed as expensive and inefficient. The building reopened in 1880 when the West Riding Constabulary took it over as the police station for the liberty of Ripon, i.e. the area outside the city. At that time there was enormous pressure to amalgamate the borough, or city, police with the county force and, in 1887, amalgamation was ordered by the Home Secretary. Kirkgate police station closed and the county police station operated from St. Marygate until 1956.[171] The old prison stood empty for some years after that, before becoming a pottery. In 1984 it opened as the Ripon Prison and Police Museum.

The gun was presented to the city by Lord Panmure in 1857 to celebrate the end of the Crimean War. It stood at the foot of the obelisk until March 1896 when, after a number of attempts to re-site, it was moved to the end of Kirkgate until scrapped as part of the Second World War effort. A similar Sebastopol cannon is displayed in Huntingdon.

Modern times

Victorian religious fervour impacted on Ripon with a flurry of new churches in the nineteenth century. Holy Trinity Church was built 1826-8 in the Early English style through the generosity of Thomas Kilvington, a Ripon doctor, who left £13,000 for 'Christian purposes'. Its fine broach spire is one of the city landmarks. The church, with galleries, offered 1,000 seats, of which 200 were to remain free of pew rents. From 1879, the church had a mission room in Allhallowgate, now occupied by the British Legion Club. In 1985, Holy Trinity crypt was cleared to provide a social and meetings area. In 2001 a scheme was developed to extend this facility and to alter the interior of the church.

After the Reformation there were reckoned to be more papists than dissenters in the town. For mass

Holy Trinity Church.

they would resort to Bishop Thornton or to some of the larger houses of the district, eg Fountains Hall. In England the pace of Roman Catholic emancipation quickened with the influx of Irish labourers in the early nineteenth century. Following the Restoration of the Hierarchy and the setting up in 1850 of a territorial episcopate with Cardinal Wiseman, termed archbishop of Westminster, the efforts of Ripon Catholics like Mrs Helen Cooper brought about the founding of St. Wilfrid's Roman Catholic parish in Ripon. From 1850, mass was said in a warehouse in Heaths Court, Low Skellgate.[172] Ordained in 1859 and serving his first mission at the chapel, Father Gordon, a former pupil of Ripon Grammar School, went on to become Bishop of Leeds. Between 1860-3 a new church, presbytery and school were built on Coltsgate Hill. It was nearly fifty years - the 12th October 1912 to be exact - before the debt was cleared and the church could be consecrated. Designed by Joseph Hansom (of the hansom cab), a devout Catholic, the church is described as being in the Lombardo Early Decorated style and is claimed to be unique, the apsidal chancel and sanctuary soaring up to a pyramid roof and bell turret. (The original design called for a baptistery to the southwest with a tower and spire above.) The first marquis of Ripon gave the lady chapel in 1878 to mark his conversion to Catholicism.

In 1818 the dissenters built a chapel, the Temple, in Allhallowgate, opposite Finkle Street, on the site of the present Temple Garden. They moved to the new 600-seat Congregational chapel on North Street in 1870, its elegant spire often visible on old postcards of the Clock Tower. The chapel closed in 1970 to become a chicken-processing plant. Hambleton Court now occupies the site.

The Clock Tower, looking towards the former Congregational chapel. Standing forty-three feet (13m) high, the Victoria Clock Tower was presented to commemorate the diamond jubilee of Queen Victoria by the Misses F. M. and C. Cross of Coney Garths, Kirkby Road. It was unveiled with much rejoicing on the 28th June 1898. Because of its effect on the flow of traffic, there have been several attempts to have it moved.

Modern times

The first Methodist New Connexion chapel in Ripon was built in 1796 down Turks Head Yard in Low Skellgate.[172] After the redbrick Early English-style chapel in Blossomgate opened in 1860, the old chapel became a warehouse. The Blossomgate building, subsequently occupied by the Zion Evangelical Baptist Church, was demolished in 2000 and a new chapel was erected on the site.

Despite frequent visits to the surrounding area, John Wesley rarely visited Ripon, because of 'the great hindrance to the work of God' in the town. The town's first Wesleyan chapel was founded in 1777 using adapted buildings on Coltsgate Hill. Wesley preached there twice, in 1780 and 1788.[173]

The Wesleyans built a new chapel, to seat nearly 1,000 worshippers, on the Coltsgate Hill site in 1861. During construction, two skeletons were discovered, side-by-side and face-to-face, about three feet (1m) from the surface; they were thought to be a male in his fifties and a female in her thirties who, 'as a result of some foul murder' had lain there for about a century, hidden under the outbuildings of a stable. The last service at Coltsgate Hill chapel took place on the 26th August 1962. Methodists continue to worship at Allhallowgate and Harrogate Road (opened in 1959).

Having broken away in 1809, the Primitive Methodists built a chapel on Priest Lane in 1821, extended twenty years later. In 1881 they moved to Allhallowgate, the new chapel seating 500, with a schoolroom for 200 attached.

The Wesleyan Mission chapel in Water Skellgate, now used by the Pentecostal Assembly of God Church, opened in 1889.

Another Nonconformist group uses premises on Church Lane, the Salvation Army has premises at Lead Lane and other religious groups meet in various public buildings around the city.

As Ripon moved into the twentieth century, church halls were used for relieving poverty. In 1892 one of the minor canons of the Cathedral successfully appealed for £2 10s (£2.50) a week to provide breakfasts for 120 poor children at Priest Lane mission three mornings a week. It was not only the children who were hungry - over 1,200 adults received bread and soup three times a week. A request that the poor passing through the city be given something from the soup kitchen was turned down to discourage tramps. The hours at Kearsley's varnish works were reduced to half past seven in the morning to half past five at night, or one o'clock on Saturdays. Kearsley's workers were fortunate: they suffered no reduction in wages. Not so the lamplighter - in 1899 the corporation reduced his wages from 10s (50p) to 7s (35p) a week.

Two years earlier, the food had been so bad that the workhouse children refused to eat their daily porridge. One citizen, Mr Hargrove, objected to the suggestion that they should be offered bread and jam on alternate days: 'Half the children of Ripon would be glad to have jam and bread', he said. He was probably right. Councillor Tom Williamson wrote to the local newspaper describing cases where 'ten human beings had been herded together in space scarcely adequate for a self respecting litter of pigs'.[174] As late as 1914, it was reported that no new houses were needed in Ripon as there were plenty vacant at rents varying from 1s 6d to 5s 6d (7.5p to 27.5p) weekly.

In 1894-5, Ripon's death-rate - 140 deaths including, out of 186 births, 81 infants under a year old - was criticised by the medical officer in his annual report as being far too high for a non-industrial town, and blamed on the overcrowded, insanitary condition of many of the old cottages crammed into the courtyards.[175] In 1892, to tackle the worst situations, orders had been issued for the rebuilding and repair of premises in Heaths Yard, Blossomgate, Fishergate, Irelands Court, Priest Lane and Stonebridgegate, and 1897 brought a plan for the demolition of the insanitary properties on the west side of Fishergate owned by Lord Ripon, to make a road through to Park Street. Five years later a tramway between Ripon Station and Studley Park was planned to follow the same route.

The contrast between the 'haves' and the 'have-nots' at that time is emphasised by the fact that 7,060 people visited Ripon on special excursion trains on August Bank Holiday 1894. But visitors were not always a blessing. The year 1904 brought complaints from the Cathedral about the increasing irreverence of visitors and their lamentable attitude to worship.[176]

With 8,225 inhabitants, the 1901 census showed an apparent increase of 711 on the 1891 count, but because of the extension of the boundaries to include Sharow and Bishopton, it actually represented a reduction in Ripon's population. The dean was appalled at the declining birth-rate and wrote to 'The Times' asserting that Canada, Australia and Africa 'can absorb all the surplus population for years to come' and asking whether such a 'willful diminution of our race' was not 'a crime against humanity and its Author'.[177]

Modern times

Soldiers arrive at Ripon Station during the First World War.

In many ways, Ripon was in a downward spiral. In 1905, a property auction closed without a single sale. A hundred blankets were distributed to the poor by the mayor; dinners for some 250 poor children were provided at the Temperance Hall at a penny each. A shed was made available in Allhallowgate where a 'working man might smoke his pipe in some degree of comfort' and, if funds could be raised, a wash-house and copper were to be provided for the poverty stricken area of Stonebridgegate.[178]

There was a hope that the Spa, opened in October 1905, would lift Ripon from the lethargy of its past, but the following year the mayor drew attention to the increasing number of children being sent to school without shoes. It was soon clear that the Spa was not going to make any significant improvement. The year 1912 was a very bad one with, nationally, the lowest potato harvest ever and a decrease in the sheep population of one and a quarter million head.[179] Emigration to Canada and Australia were up; the number of children in school fell. High unemployment was blamed on local landowners obstructing plans for industrial development. The War Office was asked to set up territorial army training camps to bolster the economy. The request was a complete reversal of a complaint to the Secretary of War a century earlier *'respecting the oppression of the Innkeepers and inhabitants of the Borough by having soldiers quartered upon them so long ... to request that [the military] may be immediately removed to some more convenient Town, more able to bear the burthen of a Regt. of soldiers quartered upon them.'*[180]

The Ripon Volunteer Rifles had been formed in February 1882. Lord de Grey had allowed the use of Red Bank for drill. Territorial army camps followed, using the same site.

The outbreak of the First World War saw the city council suggesting the setting-up of a permanent military facility. Soon, 2,000 Yorkshire Territorials and 500 workmen were billeted in the city, followed by two battalions of infantry and an army service corps, some 1,200 men and 350 horses. Approval was given for a camp, likely to become permanent, housing two divisions - some 30,000 troops - to be ready by April 1915, on a site occupying 800 to 1,000 acres (320-400ha), later extended with a 'secondary town' of some 600 acres (240ha) to the north. The main hutments of the south camp occupied the site of the old racecourse at Red Bank. Ten miles (16km) of main roads, sixteen miles (26km) of secondary roads and twelve miles (19km) of footpaths were laid, with forty-eight miles (77km) of sewers and drainpipes. A light railway ran directly into the camp from Littlethorpe siding. The camp had its own electricity generating station. Demand for water reached over 700,000 gallons (3.2 million litres) per day, completely overwhelming local supply. The face of Ripon had changed completely. The Yorkshire Post reported:

'Ripon is fast losing its air of old-world serenity and possibly for ever. There are now in fact two Ripons - the old and the new, the city and the camp. Nowhere has the war wrought a greater transformation ... the camp has a striking air of permanence.'[181]

After the war the camp reduced in size, particularly to the south, where the area was developed for housing. It came into prominence again during the World War II. Claro and Deverall barracks presently house the Royal Engineers, but with continued reductions in the armed forces, Ripon's long-term future as an army town cannot be certain.

The 'Riponians' Concert Party, First World War.

AN ILLUSTRATED HISTORY OF RIPON

Modern times

Amelia Pankhurst, the suffragette, visited Ripon in 1910 to support two suffragettes and the (unsuccessful) Liberal candidate at a meeting in the market place.

In 1913, the shop assistants pressed for a reduction in their hours from 8am to 7pm on weekdays and 8am to 10pm on Saturdays. Friday had been voluntary half-day closing. When half-day closing was made compulsory, Wednesday was suggested. (A number of the remaining privately owned shops still close on Wednesday afternoons.)

Towards the end of the nineteenth century, alcohol - 'mothers' ruin' - provided relief to large sections of the community, and the Temperance Movement was formed to help combat the problem. The drivers of the horse-drawn cabs, waiting for long hours for their fares, were particularly attracted by the warmth and shelter of alehouses and gin palaces. In London, public-spirited benefactors provided hundreds of shelters, with a stove to warm up a snack, and this

Ripon's cabmen's shelter as restored in the 1980s.

was taken up across the country. Only a small number survive. In Ripon, in 1911, Miss Sarah Carter gave a legacy of £200 in memory of her father, a former mayor, to provide Ripon's only example. It survived, albeit in a poor state, until it was rescued and restored by Ripon Civic Society in 1984. With the assistance of the Royal Engineers and financial support from the local councils, over £5,000 was spent on its restoration and maintenance. It is now in the ownership of the city council.

The first half of the twentieth century saw the end of many private specialist shops, and the rise of the multiple and the department store. Freeman, Hardy and Willis's shoe shop occupied the corner of Market Place and Westgate for almost 100 years, until the group went out of business in 1996. Hepworths clothiers: Jacksons men's outfitters; grocers Walter Willson and Moss's, have been and gone. Older Riponians remember Maurice Wards. Timothy Whites and Taylors were taken over by Boots the Chemist and amalgamated in the former Café Victoria in the 1970s. Montague Burtons arrived in 1937, joining long-established independent businesses like Harrisons stationers; Rows jewellers; Appletons pork shop; Smithsons butchers on North Street; and Harrisons on Finkle Street. With a reduced Co-operative Society on Westgate (closed 2005), and Philip Hall's department store on Fishergate, they and more recently arrived enterprises strive to survive the competition of the supermarkets. Wm Morrisons opened in the former premises of Croft & Blackburn coachbuilders (later a car showroom and garage) in September 1977; Safeway built on a green-field site on the southern outskirts of the city in 1993.

Nationally, Safeway was taken over by Morrisons and in the spring of 2004 closed the Market Place store and moved to the Safeway site. On 14th October 2004 Sainsburys opened on the former Morrison site.

The dereliction behind the west of the Market Place shops has been the focus of several efforts at re-development. Soon after the turn of the 21st century, it was announced that agreements had been reached for the transfer of land and that a new scheme was to go forward involving a new supermarket (Booths), additional shops, car parking, and a road to relieve the traffic currently flowing through the market place.

General Bernard Montgomery with Dean Owen in Ripon 1952.

Modern times

To stimulate regeneration initiatives Prince Charles visited the city and is here pictured being shown the Cathedral woodcarvings by the author.

The effect of the Arcade development, around the turn of the century, on the former bus station site was immediately to affect the commercial area, with shops re-locating to the new focus. The loss to the city's economy of the college students from 1999 was very soon apparent with numerous 'to let' signs appearing on properties - hitherto a rare occurrence.

The pattern of Ripon's vacant shops is echoed in small towns across the country: charity shops enjoy tax privileges; banks and building societies seem to predominate. Not for the first time, market traders complain of bad times. Empty stalls have appeared at the Thursday market. Out-of-town hypermarkets, attracting shoppers from long distances, affect the viability of traditional market towns like Ripon. Government policy has switched from encouraging further out-of-town shopping developments, but the trend may be irreversible and a new style of town centre may have to emerge.

Light industrial development has been encouraged to the east of the city, particularly along Dallamires Lane where, amongst garages, car showrooms and a mixture of units, chicken processing survived to the mid-1990s. Crossing Hewick Bridge, passing the sand and gravel extraction plant, the marina and the racecourse, the Boroughbridge Road entrance to the city is dominated by Econ Engineering, Wolseley Centers (Ripon's biggest employer) and builders' merchants. To fund its expansion, the college authorities encouraged the development of offices and light industrial units on its campus, but left Ripon themselves in 2001.

In the last quarter of the twentieth century, Ripon's future underwent considerable critical evaluation. Groups like the civic society, chamber of trade, tourist association, environment forum, Harrogate District Council and, latterly, Ripon Improvement Trust have produced plans and commissioned studies to find a way forward. August 2000 brought the announcement of a £3.29m Single Regeneration Budget funding to improve Ripon's prospects, creating the most positive opportunities for decades.

The reconstruction and re-organisation of Ripon Market Place of 2001 eventually came about following a draft scheme submitted by Ripon Civic Society. Following the economic loss to the city of the withdrawal of the College of Ripon and York St. John it was included in a package of measures funded under the Single Regeneration Scheme.

Modern times

Like the rest of the world, Ripon entered the 21st century not only with a great splash of celebration, but with considerable anxiety about the 'millennium bug' - computer viruses that would kick-in with the date change, and problems that would arise from computers programmed with two-digit year identification rather than four digit, i.e. 00 for 2000 would also apply to 1900. However, it passed relatively quietly and the general assumption was that, internationally, some computer companies had a vested interest in scaremongering to increase sales of protective software.

To celebrate the 400th anniversary of the granting of a charter to the town by King James I in 1604, Thursday 27th May 2004 brought the Queen and the Duke of Edinburgh to Ripon. In addition to meeting civic dignitaries, the Queen and the Duke moved amongst the crowd gathered in the market place, the focus of the visit, and chatted to stallholders, before taking lunch in the Town Hall. Previously they had visited the city to present the Royal Maundy in 1985.

Modern times

Four months after the royal visit, the Ripon Gazette announced 'Cathedral in turmoil as Dean suspended' and reported that the Very Revd. John Methuen, appointed dean of Ripon in 1995, had been 'inhibited' by the bishop from his clerical duties. Subsequently the bishop announced that an independent examiner had considered the allegations 'and decided that there is a case for the dean to answer on all twenty two formal complaints - one allegation of 'Serious, persistent or continuous neglect of duty' and twenty one allegations of *'Conduct unbecoming the office and work of a clerk in Holy Orders. A Consistory Court to determine these charges is likely to be convened later this year. (2005) The Dean is clear that he has a full answer to the complaints.'*

In the past the Minster had been thrown into turmoil by the removal of Dean Wanley from office. In 1780 he became involved in 'pecuniary difficulties' and fled the country to avoid his creditors, after which the Chapter appointed one of the canons, Robert Darley Waddilove, to look after the affairs. Waddilove was appointed Dean in 1792, after Wanley's death.

Statement on the withdrawal of charges against the Dean of Ripon

" Following a recent meeting between the Bishop of Ripon and Leeds and the Dean of Ripon, all the charges against the Dean have been withdrawn by the Promoter with the agreement of the Consistory Court and the Dean has decided to leave Ripon by the end of the year. Bishop John Packer has removed the inhibition on the Dean and welcomed his return to ministry in the Church of England. He has offered the Dean sabbatical leave between now and December 31st 2005 and the Dean has accepted that, and customary sabbatical conventions will be followed".

After twenty years of service, Alan Oliver stepped down from the post of hornblower to the city. At a time when it looked as if the tradition might come to an end for lack of volunteers, Alan took over the role and became the face of Ripon for residents and visitors alike. He proved a fine ambassador for the city and, during his tenure of the post, members of the European Nightwatchmen and Hornblowers Guild twice made official visits to the city. In September 2004 George Pickles was appointed to succeed him

Not for the first time a spate of vandalism has been affecting the city. The installation of Closed Circuit Television cameras in the city centre has had the effect of moving misbehaviour outside camera range and the Cathedral has suffered particular damage both inside and out. Traders in Kirkgate are currently campaigning for the closure of the youth café sited there. It is perhaps worth remembering that although now a museum, in the 17th century, the House of Correction on St. Marygate was established because of 'idle youths terrorising the villages'!

It is sometimes said that without history there is no future. By 2020 the vision is for Ripon to be Yorkshire's rural capital of culture and city of enterprise - a place to live, work and enjoy. Within the Ripon City Partnership, a number of working groups have been established to create a 20/20 vision for the future of Ripon. Their aim is to develop tourism; the learning environment; community awareness; to emphasize and improve the distinctive culture of Ripon; and engender a spirit of enterprise by encouraging new business ventures and the expansion of existing businesses,

The opportunity is being grasped to prepare for a future of which Ripon can be proud and the future will be our judge.

Notes

For further information, reference should be made to the Ripon Millenary Record or the Ripon Record. In the notes below the following abbreviations are used:

RMR

Ripon Millenary Record, (Harrison, Ripon, 1892)

RR

Ellis, E. Mauchline, M. Pearson, T. and Whitehead J. (Eds) A Ripon Record 1887-1986 (Phillimore, 1986)

Gowland

Gowland, T S. (1891-1983) The Antiquities of Ripon and Riponshire (Manuscript at Yorkshire Archaeological Society, Leeds.)

Thomson

Thomson, Celia. The Book of Ripon (Barracuda, 1978)

Aspects

Ripon Civic Society: Ripon: Some Aspects of its History (Dalesman, 1977)

Tuting

Tuting, John. (d1864 aged eighty) Manuscript in the Ripon Cathedral archive at the Brotherton Library, Leeds.

Hallett

Hallett, Cecil. Ripon, The Cathedral and See, (Bells Cathedral Series, 1901)

Jones

Jones, Glanville R J, 'The Ripon Estate : Landscape Into Townscape' Northern History XXXVII, December 2000

MoR I

Memorials of the Church of Saints Peter and Wilfrid, 1, (Surtees Society 74, 1882)

MoR II

Memorials of the Church of Saints Peter and Wilfrid, 2, (Surtees Society 84, 1884)

MoR III

Memorials of Ripon, Vol. 3 (Surtees Society 81, 1886).

Endnote numbers

Please see Bibliography for abbreviations.

1. Smith, D B, Principal Geologist, Institute of Geological Sciences, *Description of Rock Face at Quarry Moor*, (City of Ripon, undated paper).
2. Mayes, Atherden, Manchester and Manby, '*Yorkshire Archaeological Journal, Vol 58,* 'A Beaker Burial at West Tanfield, North Yorkshire', (Yorkshire Archaeological Society, 1986).
3. *Yorkshire Post,* 4th September 2000.
4. RR page 51.
5. RR page 146.
6. Hall, R A, *The Church Under Your Feet - Archaeological Excavations in the Crossing of Ripon Cathedral, 1997.* (York Archaeological Trust, 1998).
7. RMR Preface iv.
8. RMR page 171.
9. Ekwall, Eilert, *The Concise Oxford Dictionary of Place Names, 4th Edn.* (Oxford University Press, 1990) See also *Ripon Conservation Area* (Harrogate Borough Council. 1995).
10. *Ripon Conservation Area*, (Harrogate Borough Council, 1995)
11. Excavations by Dr Richard Hall and Mark Whyman reported at lectures to Ripon Civic and Historical Societies. See also Hall and Whyman below, and R Hall and M Whyman, 'Ripon Yarns… getting to the root of the problem', *Interim* 11, no 4, pp29-37; R.Hall, 'Ripon Yarns 2. Return to the Hill', *ibid* 12, no 3, pp 15-22 (Yorkshire Archaeological Trust, 1986-7).
12. Ekwall, E. ibid.
13. Gambles, Robert, *Yorkshire Dales Place-Names*, (Dalesman, 1995).
14. Bradley, Tom, *Yorkshire Rivers No. 8, The Ure.*(Yorkshire Post, Leeds, 1891).
15. Thomson, Celia.
16. McCutcheon, K L, *Yorkshire Fairs and Markets,* (Thoresby Society, XXXIX, 1939).
17. Foley, William Trent, *Images of Sanctity in Eddius Stephanus' Life of Bishop Wilfrid, an Early Saint's Life,* (Edwin Mellor Press, Lampeter, 1992). However, Bertram Colgrave concluded that neither the day nor the date of Wilfrid's death could be settled on present evidence. See note 55.
18. Fowler, J T. *MoR1* page 94.
19. Farrer, *Early Yorks. Charters*, I, 108-9; D. Nichol, *Thurstan: Archbishop of York* (York, 1946), page 11-15, cited by G R J Jones in 'The Ripon Estate : Landscape into Townscape' Northern History XXXVII, December 2000.
20. McKay, William. *Yorkshire Archaeological Journal* Vol 54, 'The Development of Medieval Ripon', (Yorkshire Archaeological Society, 1982).

Endnote numbers

[21] Petchey, W. (a) Lecture to Ripon Historical Society, 1992.
(b) *Ripon Historian* Vol. 1, No. 8, 'Medieval Origins of the Marketstead' (Ripon Historical Society, 1992).

[22] RMR page 24.

[23] Gowland Vol 17/13.

[24] Fiennes, Celia *Through England on a Side Saddle in the Time of William and Mary* Quoted RMR page 82.

[25] Denton, Jean *Ripon Historian* 'The Thirlway Journal' (Ripon Historical Society, 1996).

[26] RMR page 93.

[27] Forster, et al. *Ripon Cathedral its history and architecture,* (Sessions 1993).

[28] Brunskill, R W. Illustrated Handbook of Vernacular Architecture, (Faber & Faber, 1987), page167.

[29] Tuting Ms 98.

[30] Farrer, *History of Ripon* page 16.

[31] A bercary (sheep farm/house) belonging to St. Mary's Hospital is recorded on Priest Lane (Gowland 17/18).

[32] Tuting Ms.

[33] Hewlings, Richard, *Architectural History* 24, 'Ripon's Forum Populi', (1981).

[34] Gowland, 13/13.

[35] Local studies research article, (Ripon Gazette, 16th June 2000).

[36] Gowland Thomas Stockton.

[37] Ripon Town Book, section 33.

[39] Two pence for one outer door, four pence for two is the usually quoted rate (RMR) but Farrer (1806) says 'an annual tax of four pence levied upon every inhabitant, whose dwelling had but one, and of eight pence where it had two outer doors' as does Gent (1733).

[40] The Torrington diaries, ed. C Bruyn Andrews, abridged Fanny Andrews. A selection from the tours of the Hon. John Byng, later 5th Viscount Torrington between the years 1781 and 1794. (Eyre and Spottiswoode, London, 1954).

[41] Ripon Gazette Local History article 23rd June 2000; Chadwick, Anthony *Ripon Liberty* (Ripon Museum Trust, 1986).

[42] Denton, Jean, *Ripon Historian* Vol. 1 No. 8, (Ripon Historical Society, April 1992).

[43] *Aspects* page 16.

[44] Farrer. *The History of Ripon,* (1806) page 42.

[45] Denton, J & Whitehead, J K. *Ripon Historian,* (Ripon Historical Society, 1995/6); RMR, page 253.

[46] For additional information I am grateful to Mr J Lister, Secretary of Ripon Livestock Auction Mart.

[47] Wilkinson, Walter. *Puppets in Yorkshire,* (Geoffrey Bless, London, 1931).

[48] The *Life of Bishop Wilfrid* by Eddius Stephanus states thirty hides; Bede's *A History of the English Church and People* states forty hides.

[49] *Domesday Book,* [fols 303v, 380.] Cited in G R J Jones.

[50] Bede. *Life of Cuthbert* in The Age of Bede, (Penguin Classics, 1988).

[51] Kirby, D P. *St. Wilfrid at Hexham* 'Northumbria in the Time of Wilfrid', Ed. D P Kirkby, (Oriel Press, 1974).

[52] Kirby, D P. op cit.

[53] The term liberty and franchise were synonymous in medieval law and referred to a subject's right to exercise jurisdiction. 'Possession of a franchise by custom or by grant (Charter) conferred on the holder a degree of immunity, not always clearly specified, from the regular sphere of operations of the Crown's law officers; the greatest franchises were known as Palatinates. In 13th century England, the *Quo Warranto* inquiries marked one of the ways in which franchise holders came under increasing government supervision. In 1536 most privileges of franchises which had remained outside crown control were abolished by Act of Parliament, an important stage in the Tudor programme of Centralization…' Gardener & Wenborn, *The History Today Companion to British History* (Collins and Brown, 1995).

[54] Bailey, R N. *Saint Wilfrid's Crypts at Ripon and Hexham - A Visitor's Guide* (Society of Antiquaries of Newcastle upon Tyne, 1993).

[55] Eddius Stephanus. *The Life of Bishop Wilfrid,* translated by Bertram Colgrave (Cambridge University Press, 1927). I have retained Eddius Stephanus as the name of the author of the *Life of St. Wilfrid.* Readers who wish to explore the discussion of Eddius and Stephanus being separate individuals are referred to 'Bede, Eddius, Stephanus and the *Life of Wilfrid*', by D P Kirby in *English Historical Review* 98 (1983) pages 101-140.

[56] Hall, R. *The Church Under Your Feet - Archaeological Excavations in the Crossing of Ripon Cathedral,* (York Archaeological Trust, 1997).

[57] *Anglo Saxon Chronicles* page 124 trans. Anne Savage. (Tiger Books, 1995).

Endnote numbers

[58] Kirby D P op cit.

[59] Warin, Anne, *Wilfrid* (Wm Sessions, York, 1993) pages 77, 83.

[60] The Ripon tradition dates the event to c.979 AD.

[61] *The Life of Bishop Wilfrid* op cit page 186.

[62] Clearly, in the Middle Ages, both Ripon and Canterbury believed theirs to be the relics of Wilfrid I. At this distance, in the absence of any positive contradictory evidence, it would seem reasonable that the earlier and more or less contemporary account should take precedence.

[63] *The Anglo Saxons* ed. James Campbell, page 155 (Phaidon, Oxford, 1982).

[64] Trevelyan, G M. *History of England* (Longmans, 1926) page 66.

[65] Gowland Vol 7.

[66] Jones, G R J. cites MoR, I, pages 89-93.

[67] Gowland Vol 7.

[68] Kirby, Martyn. *Sanctuary - Beverley - A Town of Refuge* (Highgate Publications, Beverley, 1991).

[69] Jones, G R J. 'The Ripon Estate : Landscape into Townscape'. Details provided in advance of publication. The earlier, unpublished version differed significantly from the published edition.

[70] *Anglo-Saxon Chronicles*, trans. Anne Savage (Tiger Books, 1995).

[71] *Anglo Saxon Chronicles*, trans. Anne Savage (Tiger Books, 1995).

[72] Smith, Lucius, *The Story of Ripon Minster*, (Jackson, Leeds, 1914) page 41.

[73] Miller, J S. *Annual Report*, 'The Chapter House Range' (The Friends of Ripon Cathedral, 1984/5); Hearn, M F. *Transactions of the American Philosophical Society*, Vol. 73, part 6, 'Ripon Minster, The Beginnings of the Gothic Style in Northern England' (1983); Harrison Stuart and Barker Paul, *Journal of British Archaeological Association*, 'Ripon Minster: An Archaeological Analysis and Reconstruction of the 12th Century Church'. (1999).

[74] Dickens, A G. *The English Reformation*, (Fontana, 1967) pages 292, 300.

[75] The Hospital Foundation of Saint John The Baptist, church leaflet.

[76] *The Tourist's Companion*, (Langdale, Ripon, 1818).

[77] *The Tourist's Companion*, op cit p.,15

[78] RMR page 177.

[79] RR page 12.

[80] Hearn, M F, op cit 1983; Harrison & Barker, op.cit 1999.

[81] Gowland Vol. 2 page 52, Vol. 13 page 3.

[82] Gowland

[83] Hallett, Cecil. *Ripon: The Cathedral and See,* (London, George Bell, 1909) page 21.

[84] This is referred to in John Leland's itinerary.

[85] Smith, Lucius, *The Story of Ripon Minster,* (1914).

[86] Mauchline, M. *Aspects.*

[87] Gilyard-Beer, R *Yorkshire Archaeological Journal,* 58 'Bedern Bank and the Bedern, Ripon', (Yorkshire Archaeological Society, 1986).

[88] Tracy, Charles. *English Gothic Choir-Stalls 1400-1540* (Boydell Press, 1990); see also Purvis, Rev J S, *The use of Continental woodcuts and prints by the 'Ripon School' of Woodcarvers in the early sixteenth century* (Society of Antiquaries, 1936).

[89] *Visitors' Guide to Ripon and Fountains Abbey* (Thirlway & Son, c.1892) page 50. The canopy was made by Archer of Oxford and cost £200. It currently stands at the western end of the north aisle in the area known as the Consistory Court but the area is scheduled for re-organisation.

[90] *Survey of Chantries,* (Surtees Society, Vol. XCII Part II, 1895).

[91] See *Lewis Carroll's Ripon* by Maurice H Taylor.

[92] Hall, R A, and Whyman, Mark. *Medieval Archaeology Vol. XL,* 'Settlement and Monasticism at Ripon, North Yorkshire from the 7th to 11th Centuries AD' (1996), The authors suggest that the market place was sited along the course of a route originally linking Kirkgate with North Street.

[93] Re-drawn from Fieldhouse, Roger. *Group Projects in Local History,* ed. Alan Rogers, 'The Hearth Tax and Other Records' (Dawson/National Institute of Adult Education, 1977), page 85.

[94] Mauchline M, *Aspects.*

[95] RR page 47.

[96] Tuting page 74.

[97] Defoe, Daniel. *A Tour Through England and Wales.*

[98] Aspects page 54.

[99] For the information on roads following the enclosures I am indebted to a dissertation *The Enclosure of the Common Lands of Ripon during the C18th and C19th* by J M Haigh, Ripon College, May 1968.

[100] RR 147, 150, 152.

[101] RR 163.

[102] *Ripon Gazette* 12th January 1996.

[103] RR pages 27-28.

[104] Walbran, page 57.

Endnote numbers

[105] Jones, P E. *A Short History of the Ure Navigation,* (Ripon Motor Boat Club, 1986); RMR page 104.

[106] MoR1 page 202.

[107] Gowland Vol. 17.

[108] Jones, G R J. page 14.

[109] Duchy of Lancaster 11E07(A) - 07 1782.

[110] Much of this information is drawn from papers by Cyril Mason, WEA class, 1994 and J M Haigh, Ripon College 1968.

[111] RMR page 9; Victoria County History (Yorkshire) page 433.

[112] Gowland 13/18.

[113] Jones, G R J. page 30.

[114] Batchelor, R E. *Yorkshire's Early History,* (Advertiser Press, Huddersfield, 1973) page 75.

[115] *Aspects* pages 26, 28.

[116] *Aspects* page 16.

[117] Information based on an article in *The Dalesman* August 1983 by Carson I A Ritchie. See also Longbottom, S H. *Ripon Lace making,* (Dalesman, October, 1956); Howard, Stanley. 'The Lace makers of Ripon', (The Ridings, February 17th 1965) pages 34-37.

[118] Williams, Ann. *Country Crafts in Yorkshire* (Dalesman, 1970).

[119] Thirlway, *Visitors Guide to Ripon.*

[120] Local studies research article, (*Ripon Gazette,* 8th September 2000).

[121] RR page 117.

[122] *Aspects* page 71.

[123] Baines *History, Directory and Gazetteer of the County of York.*

[124] Blakeborough, J Fairfax. *The History of Yorkshire Racing* (F Johnson Sporting Publications). My thanks to Mr Michael Hutchinson for drawing this to my attention.

[125] RMR page 158.

[126] *Thirlway Journal.*

[127] For this information I am indebted to the late Mrs Jean Potts of the Wilfrid Festival Committee.

[128] Farrer, W. *History of Ripon,* (1806).

[129] Jacob, Naomi. *Me Again.*

[130] Blakeborough, R. *Yorkshire Wit, Character, Folklore and Customs,* (1911), page 113.

[131] Williams, Mary. *Witches in old North Yorkshire,* (Hutton Press, 1987).

[132] *Gentlemen's Magazine,* August 1790, quoted in *The History of Ripon Minster,* by Lucius Smith.

[133] RR page 154

[134] *Gentlemen's Magazine,* 1790, quoted in Brand's Popular Antiquities.

[135] Ministri were "inferior", or lower status, ministers or servants of the minister; cf. the canons who were 'superior' or senior ministers.

[136] Leeds Mercury, 1833.

[137] Thompson, E P. *Customs in Common,* (London, Merlin Press, 1991).

[138] Chadwick, Anthony. *Ripon Liberty.* (Ripon Museum Trust, 1986) page 20.

[139] Pearson, E. *Annual Report,* 'The Select Vestry of Churchwardens of Ripon Cathedral Parish' (Friends of Ripon Cathedral, 1999).

[140] Tate, W.E. *The Parish Chest,* (Cambridge University Press, 1946).

[141] Chadwick, Anthony. Ripon Historian Vol.4 No. 8 *The Case of a Missing Vestry,* (Ripon Historical Society, Oct. 2000).

[142] Jackson, George. *The Wakeman,* 'Some Old Ripon Play Bills', (July, 1950).

[143] Holmes, R S. *The Wakeman,* 'History of Yorkshire County Cricket, 1833-1903' (June, 1952).

[144] Hallett, page 30.

[145] Lawson, J, & Silver H. *A Social History of Education in England,* (London, Methuen, 1973) page 242.

[146] Gordon, Colin. *Beyond the Looking Glass,* (Hodder & Stoughton, 1982) page 28.

[147] RR page 63.

[148] Roach, John. *Yorkshire Schools in the First Half of the Nineteenth Century,* (Yorkshire Archaeological Journal, 2000).

[149] Smith, Percival. *The Jepson Story,* (Jepson's Educational Foundation, 1966).

[150] *The Story of Skellfield School* 1877-1927 (Skellfield School).

[151] McGregor, G P A. *Church College for the 21st Century* (Sessions, York, 1991) page 21.

[152] Collier, Alice. *Alice's Story,* ed. Taylor, M H, (Ripon Civic Society, 1991).

[153] Walbran, J R. *Guide to Ripon.*

[154] Jones, W D *Prosperity Robinson,* (McMillan, London, 1967).

[155] Rogers, P W. *A History of Ripon Grammar School,* (Wakeman Press, Ripon 1954); Harris, J, and Snodin, M. *Sir William Chambers, Architect to George III,* (Yale, 1997). There is some disagreement about the date of Chambers leaving Ripon Grammar School. Rogers says it was 1746; Harris & Snodin say 'when he was 17'.

[156] Rogers, P W. ibid.

Endnote numbers

[157] Kellett, Arnold, *Historic Knaresborough,* (Smith Settle, Otley, 1991).

[158] Jacob, Naomi. *Me, Likes and Dislikes,* (Hutchinson, 1954).

[159] Sullivan, Dick, *Navvyman*.

[160] Schaaf, Larry *History of Photography* Vol. 3, No. 4, October 1979, 'Charles Piazzi Smyth's 1865 Conquest of the Great Pyramid',

[161] Crompton, R E J. *Reminiscences,* (Constable, 1928); *Ripon Gazette* 28th July 2000.

[162] RMR page 157.

[163] Gowland states: 'In 1836, the See of Ripon was established, but the substitution of the name "City" for "Borough" does not date from this change, it was a dignity inserted in and possibly created by the City of Ripon Act of 1865, an Act to enable the Corporation to complete the purchase of the Gas works and incidentally now repealed.' (Vol 13, Part IV).

[164] RMR page 158.

[165] RR page 45.

[166] Thompson, Beryl. *Vagrancy* (Ripon Museum Trust, 1996); Ridley, Jasper. The Tudor Age, (Guild, 1988).

[167] Chadwick, Anthony. *Yorkshire Workhouses,* (Ripon Museum Trust, 1996).

[168] Thompson, Beryl op cit.

[169] Chadwick, Anthony, *Ripon Liberty,* (Ripon Museum Trust, 1986).

[170] RMR pages 178 and 229.

[171] I owe much of the section on police and prisons to Dr John Whitehead.

[172] RMR pages 116, 182, 184.

[173] RMR pages 108 and Collins, Rachel, *Reasons for the Closing Down of Coltsgate Hill Wesleyan Chapel,* (Ripon Civic Society competition essay, 1987).

[174] RR page 15.

[175] RR page 7.

[176] RR page 26.

[177] RR page 21.

[178] RR page 28.

[179] RR page 43.

[180] RMR page 123.

[181] RR page 49 gives a concise account of the development.

Appendix 1 - Maps and Plans

The following, whilst not claiming to list every map that relates to Ripon, may help the reader who wishes to trace a particular geographical detail:

1577	Christopher Saxton (Yorkshire)
1600	Robert Greenhurst (lordship of Kirkby Malzeard - includes detail of western boundary)
1610	John Speed (Yorkshire)
1675	John Ogilby (road map)
1720	Owen-Bowen (road map)
1733	Gent/Parker (earliest Ripon town plan so far traced)
1747	Richard Beckwith (enclosures)
1772	Thomas Jefferys (in addition to his general map of the area, there is a detailed Ripon town plan on his map of the Environs of Muker, Lune and Stainmore Forest)
1800	John Humphries (enclosure awards)
1818	T Langdale
1827	John Wood - Ripon Cathedral Archive
1831	Cooper survey - (Parliamentary Returns) - copy at Yorkshire Archaeological Society, Leeds)
1842	Thomas Moule (Yorkshire - includes early railways)
1854	Ordnance Survey
1892/3	Ordnance Survey
1909	Ordnance Survey
1925	Vyner Estate (at Sheepscar Archive)
1983	Ordnance Survey
1995	Ordnance Survey

Many of these maps may be viewed at Ripon Library. Others are available at North Yorkshire County Archives, Northallerton, or Yorkshire Archaeological Society, Leeds. Ripon Cathedral Archive is at the Brotherton Library, Leeds.

Appendix 2 - Street names

pn = personal name   OE = old English   ON = old Norse

From 1900 all streets, if not already, were to be named and numbered.

Present	Medieval Spelling	Earliest Record	Meaning
Ailcey Hill	Elueshov, -howe	1228	Elf's mound
Allhallowgate	Alhalgh(e)gate	1307	Street of Church of All Hallows
Aismunderby	Asmundrebi	1086	pn. Asmundr (ON) farmstead/village
Bedern Bank	Bedernbank(e) (le)	1369	Prayer house or chapel bank
Barefoot Street	Berfotgate	1307	Barley ford
Bishopton	Biscoptun	1030	Bishops farmstead (OE)
Blossomgate	Plaxomgate	1228	Possibly Plough-swain street
Bondgate	Bondegate	1228	Bondsman/peasant street
Borrage Green/Lane	Burghwage (le)	1377	From 'burgage'
Clotherholme	Cludun	1086	At the rocks (OE)
	Coltestakes }	1533	Stakes to which colts tethered
Coltsgate Hill	Cowsgate Hill }	1771	
	Cornhill (lost)		
	Corn(e)hill (le)	1340	Hill where corn was sold
Coney Garth	Cunyngarth	1457	Warren
Deep Ghyll	Dep(e)gil(e), -gyll	1315	Deep pool ravine
Fishergate	Fisshegate	1549	Street where fish was sold
Hell Wath		1673	Flat stone ford
Horsefair	Hors(e)fair(e) (le)	1367	Where horse sales were held
Kirkgate	Kyrk(e)gate (le)	c.1234	Church street
Market Place	Merkedstede (le)	1281	
Mulwith	Mulewath	1170	pn Mulis ford (from ON)
New Row (lost)	New(e)Raw(e)	1454	Now King Street
North Lees	North Lathes	1321	North barns
Priest Lane	Prestelane	1419	Priests clearing
Quarry Moor	Quarlemoor.	1316	
St. Agnesgate	Annus(e)gate	1228	From street of the hospital of St. Anne
Sharow	Sharou	1114	Boundary hill
Skellgate, High & Low	Skelgate, -gatt	1228	Street leading to the R Skell
Skittergate gutter	Skyteryk	1228	A sewer
St. Marysgate	Stammergate	1771	? From 'chapelle of our Lady' - Santa Maria - Sta.Ma
Shambles (lost)	Fleshamels (le)	1345	Where (esp.) meat is sold
Stonebridgegate	Stayn(e)briggegate	1228	Street leading to the stone bridge
Stammergate	Staynemergate	1453	Corruption of above but see 'St. Marygate'
Westgate	Westgat' (le)	1228	West way
Whitcliffe	Hwiteclyf	1235	White bank

Appendix 3 - Market Place Facts

12thC	Planned market place is laid out.
1306	Archbishop forbids markets to be held in the church.
1441	Affray between archbishop's men and king's tenants of forest of Knaresborough over Ripon Fair.
1569	Catholics muster their troops before marching to defeat -Rising of the North.
c.1600	'Wakemans House' re-fronted to face square.
1611	Market cross moved.
1642	Puritan forces defeated in the market place by force from Skipton Castle.
1702	The market place paved, new cross (obelisk) and pillory erected.
1781	Market cross rebuilt.
1800	Town Hall built as the assembly rooms.
1856	Water tank installed 6000 gallons (27,000l).
1859	Clock fixed to Town Hall.
1858	Cattle and sheep fairs moved to Treasurers Garth. Crimean War cannon placed at foot of Obelisk to 1896.
1861	Cattle and sheep fairs moved back to market square.
1873	Drinking fountain installed (to 1895).
1881	Cattle auction moves to North Street - Brewster Terrace area (?).
1882	Four stone crosses around the obelisk replaced by six Brays lamps.
1886	Inscription painted on Town Hall.
1892	Mechanics institute (now post office) built.
1895	Fountain removed.
1895	Death of last city watchman; up to 1876 the watchmen had set off hourly from sentry boxes at each side of the market place.
1895-1906	Road-widening schemes for Fishergate, Queen Street and Westgate.
1897	Twelve trees planted by former mayors.
1897	Town Hall presented to city by marquis of Ripon.
1898	Order banning sale of sheep, cattle and swine withdrawn - north side of the market place concreted.
1899	Public lavatories constructed, demolished 2001.
1899	To reduce costs the gas company replaced the six Brays gas lamps with four Kitson oil lamps.
1899	St. Wilfrid statue placed on new premises of Knaresborough & Claro Bank.
1899-1904	Middle Street demolished.
1900	Cobbles concreted over.

Appendix 3 - Market Place Facts

1903	Moss's shop demolished for Westgate road-widening - Freeman Hardy & Willis take the remainder of site to 1996. A cupola stood on top of the building from 1904-1950s.
1903	Cattle market confined to south corner of the square.
1904	First omnibus in Ripon.
1905	Crown Hotel licence given up - becomes Croft & Blackburns Garage and Carriage Works, from 1977 Morrisons Supermarket. The old inn sign survives.
1911	Cabmen's shelter provided.
1912	Change of site for cattle market resisted; water trough provided.
1913	Shop assistants seek reduced hours from 8am-7pm on Weekdays and 8am-10pm on Saturdays.
1915	Half-day fixed at Wednesday (optional Saturday).
1921	Hire of stalls losing money - fierce opposition to increased charges for stalls selling manufactured goods. Little extra revenue raised.
1932	Decline in income from market continues.
1946	Thirlways shop demolished (next to 'Wakemans House') - top of High Skellgate.
2001	Market Place regeneration scheme.

Appendix 4 - Bibliography

Ripon Millenary Record (RMR), (Harrison, Ripon, 1892).

Historic Ripon : *The City & The Cathedral,* (G Parker, Ripon, c1900).

The Tourist's Companion 1818: A Guide to Ripon etc., (St. Margaret's Bookshop (reprint), 1972).

The History of Ripon, (Farrer, 1806).

Baines, H W. *Have Handcart Will Travel,* (H W Baines, 1994).

Bede. *History of the English Church & People,* (ed. L Sherley Price) (Penguin, 1955).

Bell, G. (ed) *Yorkshire Field Studies,* (University of Leeds Institute of Education, 1967).

Clark, Ann. *The Real Alice,* (Michael Joseph, 1981).

Chadwick, A. *Ripon Liberty : Law & Order over the last 300 years,* (Ripon Museum Trust, 1986).

Denton, J (ed). *The Thirlway Journal: A Record of Life in early Victorian Ripon,* (Ripon Historical Society, c1995).

Forster, W etc. *Ripon Cathedral : Its History and Architecture,* (Wm Sessions, York, 1993).

Fowler, J T (Ed), *Memorials of Ripon I,* Surtees Society, LXXIV, Durham, 1881) (MoRI).

Fowler, J T (Ed), *Memorials of Ripon II,* Surtees Society, LXXXIV, Durham, 1884) (MoRII).

Fowler, J T (Ed), *Memorials of Ripon III,* Surtees Society, LXXXI, Durham, 1886) (MoRIII).

Fremantle, W H. *Presentation of the Town Hall to the City of Ripon,* (William Harrison, Ripon, 1897).

Gent, Thomas. *Ancient & Modern History of the Loyal Town of Ripon,* (1733).

Gott, Jim. *Bits & Blots of t'owd Spot: Memories of Ripon 1900-1950,* (Kelvin H Gott & Crakehill Press, Thirsk, 1986).

Gowland, T S. *The Antiquities of Ripon and Riponshire.*

Hall, R A. *Interim* 'Ripon Yarns : 1/2 : Anglo Saxon Ripon', (York Archaeological Trust, 1986/7).

Hall, R A. *Yorkshire Monasticism. Archaeology, Art & Architecture from the 7th to 16th Centuries,* ed. I. R. Hoey, 'Antiquaries & Archaeology in and around Ripon Minster', (British Archaeological Association Transactions XVI, 1995).

Hall R A & Whyman, Mark. *Medieval Archaeology Vol. XL,* 'Settlement and Monasticism at Ripon, North Yorkshire from the 7th to 11th Centuries AD', (1996).

Hallett, Cecil. *Ripon: The Cathedral and See,* (Bell's Cathedral Series 1901).

Harrison, S and Barker P. *Journal of the British Archaeological Association,* 'Ripon Minster: An archaeological analysis and Reconstruction of the 12th Century Church', (1999).

Hearn M F. *Ripon Minster The Beginning of the Gothic Style in Northern England,* American Philosophical Society, Philadelphia, 1983.

Jones, G R J. *Northern History XXXCII* 'The Ripon Estate: Landscape into Townscape', Leeds University, 2000.

Jones, G R J. *Leeds & its Environs : Geographical essays,* 'Historical Geography of Settlement in Yorkshire Dales', (Leeds University, 1985).

Kitching, L. *The Church of Ripon in the Later Middle Ages,* MA Thesis, Manchester, 1939.

McGregor, G P A. *A Church College for the 21st Century? 150 years of Ripon & York St. John,* (University College of Ripon & York St. John, 1991).

Ripon Civic Society. *A Ripon Record 1887-1986,* (Phillimore 1986) (RR).

Appendix 4 - Bibliography

Ripon Civic Society. *Ripon : Some Aspects of its History,* (1972) (Aspects).

Ripon Civic Society. *Ripon in Old Picture Postcards,* (European Library, Holland, 1985).

Ripon Historical Society. *Hearth Tax List for Claro Wapentake 1692* (1990).

Rogers, P W. *A History of Ripon Grammar School,* (Harrison, Ripon, 1954).

Smith, A H. *The Place Names of the West Riding of Yorkshire,* (Cambridge University Press, 1961).

Smith, Lucius. *The Story of Ripon Minster,* (Jackson, Leeds, 1914).

Stephanus, Eddius. *Life of Bishop Wilfrid,* (ed. B Colgrave,), (Cambridge University Press 1927).

Taylor, M H. (ed). *Alice's Story: This was my Childhood,* (Ripon Civic Society, 1991).

Taylor, M H. *Lewis Carroll's Ripon,* (M H Taylor, Ripon, 1998).

Thomson, Celia. *The Book of Ripon* (Barracuda, 1978).

Tuting, J. Manuscript in the Ripon Cathedral archive. Brotherton Library, Leeds. C19th.

Walbran, J R. *Guide to Ripon* 1862, (G H Smith, Easingwold reprint 1972).

Wilkinson, A M. *Ripon Training College: The First Hundred Years,* (The College, Ripon, 1963).

Appendix 5 - Mayors of Ripon

1604-5	Hugh Ripley (Merchant and mercer)	1637-38	Wilfrid Sanderson
1605-6	Anthony Taylor	1638-39	Thomas Redshaw
1606-7	Henry Snowe	1639-40	William Holmes (Draper)
1607-8	William Fawcett	1640-41	Richard Mawtus / Maultass
1608-9	George Pulleyn	1641-42	Thomas Cundall
1609-10	Wm Cooke alias Applebie (Tanner)	1642-43	Eeonard Thompson
1610-11	Roger Holmes	1643-44	Miles Moodie
1611-12	Thomas Cundall	1644-45	Ralph Warwick (Draper)
1612-13	Thomas Wardroper	1645-46	Nicholas Kitchin (Grocer)
1613-14	William Battie	1646-47	Sampson Cowper (Merchant and mercer)
1614-15	John Greene	1647-48	John Jefferson (Draper)
1615-16	Francis Thekeston (Solicitor)	1648-49	William Newell
1616-17	Hugh Ripley	1696-97	Thomas Craven (Grocer)
1617-18	Simon Brown (Dyer)	1697-98	John Strother (Mercer)
1618-19	Joseph Burton (Haberdasher and felt maker)	1698-99	William Myers
1819-20	Anthony Taylor	1699-00	William Chambers (Apothecary)
1620-21	James Thompson	1700-01	Charles Lister (Mercer)
1621-22	Edward Kirkby	1701-02	John Sedgwick
1622-23	Wm Battie, Jnr (Merchant)	1702-03	John Aislabie Esq.
1623-24	Ralph Warwick	1703-04	Thomas Charnock (Draper)
1624-25	John Hartley	1704-05	Stephen Palliser (Tanner)
1625-26	Miles Moodie	1705-06	George Pinckney (Mercer)
1626-27	Thomas Redshaw	1706-07	Cuthbert Chambers (Apothecary)
1627-28	Thomas Topham	1707-08	Roger Wright
1627-28	Miles Moodie	1708-09	Thos Jackson (Woollen draper)
1628-29	Miles Percivall	1709-10	Wm Chambers (Apothecary)
1629-30	Leonard Thompson (Draper)	1710-11	John Ripley (Grocer)
1630-31	Hugh Ripley	1711-12	Chris.Braithwaite (Mercer)
1631-32	William Cooke	1712-13	Johnson Wood (Grocer)
1632-33	Thomas Cundall	1713-14	Henry Green (Tanner)
1633-34	James Thompson	1714-15	Charles Lister (Mercer)
1634-35	Ralph Warwick	1715-16	John Sedgwick
1635-36	Edward Wright	1716-17	Thomas Burton (Grocer)
1636-37	Bartholomew Kettlewell (Mercer)	1717-18	Willm Horner (Whitesmith)

Appendix 5 - Mayors of Ripon

1718-19	Christopher Wayne
1719-20	Christopher Hunton (Sadler)
1720-21	Charles Oxley (Surgeon)
1721-22	Richard Cundall
1722-23	John Charnock
1723-24	Jas Jackson (Woollen draper)
1724-25	William Aislabie (Esq)
1725-26	Stephen Palliser
1726-27	George Pinckney (Mercer)
1727-28	John Horner
1728-29	Charles Lister
1729-30	William Horner (Whitesmith)
1730-31	Christopher Wayne
1731	Charles Oxley (Surgeon)
1732	Simon Hutchinson (Apothecary)
1733	John Charnock
1734-35	George Loup (Apothecary and surgeon)
1735-36	Stephen Palliser (Tanner)
1736-37	Jas Jackson (Woollen draper)
1737-38	John Wilson (Grocer)
1738-39	Charles Oxley (Apothecary and surgeon)
1739-40	James Horner (Clockmaker)
1740-41	William Aislabie (Esq.)
1741-42	William Chambers (Surgeon and apothecary)
1742-43	Thomas Broadbelt (Grocer)
1743-44	John Lister (Mercer)
1744-45	William Theakstone
1745-46	Edmund Braithwaite (Surgeon)
1746-47	John Horner (Grocer)
1747-48	Simon Hutchinson (Apothecary)
1748-49	George Loup (Pothecry and surgeon)
1749-50	Henry Kirkby
1750-51	Geo. Charnock (Bridle cutter)
1751-52	John Wilson (Grocer)
1752-53	Christr Braithwaite (Mercer and woollen draper)
1753-54	William Thompson (Apothecary)
1754-55	James Horner (Clockmaker)
1755-56	Matt. Beckwith (Bookseller)
1756-7	John Lister (Mercer)
1757-58	John Hutchinson (Apothecary and surgeon)
1758-59	William Askwith (Brewer)
1759-60	Richard Grainge (Grocer)
1760-61	Edw. Ayrton (Barber Chirurgeon)
1761-62	William Grimston (Grocer)
1762-63	John Terry (Spurrier)
1763-64	William Theakstone
1764-65	Henry Kirkby
1765-66	Geo. Charnock (Bridle cutter)
1766-67	Christr Braithwaite (Mercer and woollen draper)
1767-68	Matt. Beckwith (Bookseller)
1768-69	William Lawrence (Esq)
1769-70	William Askwith (Brewer)
1770-71	John Hutchinson (Apothecary and surgeon)
1771-72	Charles Allanson (Esq)
1772-73	William Grimston (Grocer)
1773-74	John Terry (Spurrier)
1774-75	Peter Horner
1775-76	Thomas Walker (Grocer)
1776-77	Thomas Horner (Coach maker)
1777-78	William Robinson (Apothecary)
1778-79	Richard Beckwith (Bookseller)
1779-80	Chris. Braithwaite (Mercer)
1780-81	John Hutchinson (Apothecary)
1781-82	Thomas Wilkinson (Spirit merchant)

1782-83	William Askwith (Brewer)	1815-16	James Britain (Brewer)
1783-84	William Grimston (Grocer)	1817-17	William Morton (Land Agent)
1784-85	Wm Bell (Surgeon apothecary)	1817-18	Willey Edwd Carter (Watch maker and Jeweller)
1785-86	Hon. Fredck Robinson (MP)		
1786-87	John Terry (Spurrier)	1818-19	Joseph Beevers Terry (Banker)
1787-88	Thomas Walker (Grocer)	1819-20	John Britain (Grocer)
1788-89	Thomas Horner (Coach Maker)	1820-21	Peter Wright (Mercer)
1789-90	Willm Robinson (Apothecary)	1821-22	Ralph Heslop (Wine Merchant)
1790-91	Richard Beckwith (Bookseller)	1822-23	William Pearson (Currier)
1791-92	John Hutchinson (Apothecary and Surgeon)	1823-24	William Farrer (Bookseller)
		1824-25	Reuben Raw (Wine and Spirit merchant)
1792-93	Thomas Wilkinson (Spirit Merchant)	1825-26	Richd Johnson (Watchmaker)
1793-4	Thomas Terry (Banker and Grocer)	1826-27	George Snowden (Mercer)
1794-95	John Ewbank (Butcher)	1827-28	James Britain (Brewer)
1795-96	William Grimston (Grocer)	1828-29	William Morton (Land Agent)
1796-97	William Bell (Surgeon)	1830	Joseph Beevers Terry (Banker)
1797-98	John Stevenson (Mercer)	1831	John Britain Grocer
1798-99	William Atkinson (Timber Merchant)	1832-33	Christopher Nelson (Grocer)
1799-1800	William Downing	1833-34	Ralph Heslop (Wine merchant)
1800-01	Robert Shaw (Sadler)	1834-35	Jas Moore Bowman (Surgeon)
1801-02	John Pearson (Banker)	1835-36	Thomas Judson (Druggist)
1802-03	Thomas Wilkinson	1836	John Willey (Linen Draper)
1803-04	William Colbeck (Cooper)	1836-37	Quintin Rhodes (Solicitor)
1804-05	John Britain (Grocer)	1837-38	William Pearson (Currier)
1805-06	William Theakston (Stocking Weaver)	1838-39	Christopher Horn (Draper)
1806-07	John Fairgray (Hotel Proprietor)	1839-40	Thos. Wright Linen Draper
1807-08	Peter Wright (Mercer)	1886-87	John Baynes
1808-09	John Rawson (Builder)	1887-88	John Baynes
1809-10	Thomas Terry (Banker and Grocer)	1888-89	H. Mann Thirlway
1810-11	John Ewbank (Bucher)	1889-90	Thomas Hargrave
1811-12	John Stevenson (Mercer)	1890-91	Thomas Smithson
1812-13	Reuben Raw (Wine and Spirit merchant)	1891-92	Thomas Smithson
1813-14	William Farrer (Bookseller)	1892-93	Joseph Brooks Parkin
1814-15	Richard Johnson (Watch maker)	1893-94	Francis Smith

Appendix 5 - Mayors of Ripon

1894-95	John Baynes		1916-17	Frederick William Hargrave
1895-96	1st Marquess of Ripon		1917-18	Frederick William Hargrave
1896-97	Thomas Williamson		1918-19	Frederick William Hargrave
1897-98	John Banks Lee		1919-20	George Hotham New ton
1898-99	Arthur Wells		1920-21	George Hotham Newton
1899-1900	Richard Wilkinson		1921-22	Walter Fennel
1900-01	John Spence		1922-23	William Hemsworth
1901-02	John Spence		1923-24	William Hemsworth
1881-82	George Kearsley (Engineer)		1924-25	William Hemsworth
1882-83	John Banks Lee (Draper)		1925-26	Charles Harker
1883-84	Henry Cecil Bickersteth (Varnish manufacturer)		1926-27	Charles Harker
			1927-28	Thomas Fowler Spence
1884-85	John Banks Lee (Draper)		1928-29	Thomas Fowler Spence
1885-86	John Baynes (Slate merchant)		1929-30	Sidney George Moss
1886-87	John Baynes		1930-31	John Proudfoot
1887-88	John Baynes		1931-32	John Proudfoot
1888-89	Henry Mann Thirlway (Printer)		1932-33	Richard Thorpe
1889-90	Thomas Hargrave (Saddletree maker)		1933-34	Richard Thorpe
1890-91	Thomas Smithson (Butcher and farmer)		1934-35	William Russell Dixon
1891-92	Thomas Smithson		1935-36	William Russell Dixon
1902-03	William Topham Moss		1936-37	John Ireland McHenry
1903-04	William Topham Moss		1937-38	John Ireland McHenry
1904-05	John Banks Lee		1938-39	Frederick Isaac Trees
1905-06	George Simpson		193940	Frederick Isaac Trees
1906-07	John Banks Lee		1940-41	Frederick Isaac Trees
1907-08	Herbert Morris Bower		1941-42	Margaret Sara Steven (Nov.-May)
1908-09	Herbert Morris Bower		194142	William Russell Dixon (June-Oct.)
1909-10	Francis George Metcalfe		1942-43	Arthur Nettleton
1910-11	Walter Fennel		1943-44	Arthur Nettleton
1911-12	Walter Fennel		1944-45	Leavens Marson King
1912-13	Walter Fennel		1945-46	William Russell Dixon
1913-14	Thomas Harrison (Nov.. Dec.)		1946-47	William Russell Dixon
1914-15	Edward Taylor		1947-48	William H. Clayden
1915-16	Frederick William Hargrave		1948-49	William H. Clayden (Nov.-May)

1949-50	Frank Charles Lowley		1983-84	John Briscoe Briscombe
1950-51	Frank Charles Lowley		1984-85	John McGarr
1951-52	Frank Charles Lowley		1985-86	John Thompson
1952-53	William Maylott Eccles		1986-87	Rowland Simpson
1953-54	William Maylott Eccles		1987-88	Rowland Simpson
1954-55	Cecil Augustus Fearn		1988-89	James Simpson
1955-56	Cecil Augustus Feam		1989-90	John Baslington
1956-57	William Norman Wells		1990-91	Bernard Derbyshire
1957-58	William Davies Toulman		1991-92	Robert Britton
1958-59	William Davies Toulman		1992-93	Mrs Doreen Spence
1959-60	Walter Roy Beaumont		1993-94	Miss Constance Birkinshaw
1960-61	James Miles Coverdale		1994-95	Harold Baynes
1961-62	James Miles Coverdale		1995-96	Joseph Cooper
1962-63	Cecil Augustus Fearn		1996-97	Robert Britton
1963-64	Wilfrid Henry Parnaby		1997-98	John Groves
1964-65	Wilfrid Henry Parnaby		1998-99	Barry Kay
1965-66	Neville Stephenson		1999-2000	Alan Skidmore
1966-67	Neville Stephenson		2000-01	Paul Freeman
1967-68	Frederick Walter Spence		2001-02	David Harrison
1968-69	Frederick Walter Spence		2002-03	Bernard Bateman
1969-70	Luigi George Handel Feather		2003-04	David Pamaby
1970-71	Luigi George Handel Feather		2004-05	Stuart Martin
1971-72	Norman Wilfrid Pollard			
1972-73	Walter Roy Beaumont			
1973-74	Walter Jack Baily			
1974-75	Edward Iver Jones			
1975-76	John Henry Richmond			
1976-77	Michael Frederick Falkingham			
1977-78	John McGarr			
1978-79	Frederick Walter Spence			
1979-80	Walter Jack Baily			
1980-81	Barrie Price			
1981-82	Robert Winster Bracken			
1982-83	Walter Roy Beaumont			

Appendix 6 - Bishops of Ripon

(Bishops of Ripon and Leeds from 2000)

Eadhead	681-686
Charles Longley	1836-1856
Robert Bickersteth	1857-1884
William Boyd-Carpenter	1884-1912
Thomas Drury	1912-1920
Thomas Strong	1920-1926
Edward Burroughs	1926-1935
Geoffrey Lunt	1935-1946
Geoffrey Chase	1946-1959
John Moorman	1959-1976
Stuart Price	1976-1977
David Young	1977-1999
John Packer	2000-

Appendix 7 - Members of Parliament for Ripon

Extracted from Ripon Millenary Appendix pxii for which see details of members

Monarch	Date	Returned	Other candidates
Edward I	1295	John de Stapleford f John de Eborum	
	1299	. . . ton . . . .thorpe	
		(names obliterated except for final syllable)	
Edward II	1307	Hugo de Skalton Rogerus de Clotherum	
	1309	Summoned but names not known if any returned	
	1325	Summoned but names not known if any returned	
Edward III	1337	Richard de Stow Richard de Dystynby Richard Aldereth	
Mary	1553	Marmaduke Wyvill Edward Beyseley	
	1554	William Restall John Temple	
Philip and Mary	1555	John Holmes Thomas Poleye	
	1537	William Hethe Thomas Leweknor	
Elizabeth	1558-9	No return from Ripon	
	1562-3	George Leighe Richard Pratt	
	1572	Martin Birkhead John Scott	
	1585	Martin Birkhead Gervase Lee	
	1586	William Spencer Samuel Sands	
	1599	Peter Yorke William Smyth	
	1592	Anthony Wingfield William Bennet	
	1597	John Bennett, EL.D Christopher Perkins, EL.D	
	1601	Christopher Perkins LL.D John Thornebroughe	
James I	1603	John Mallory John Bennett LL.D	
	1614	Thomas Vavasor Sir William Mallory	
	1620	Sir William Mallory	
		Sir Thomas Posthumus Hoby	
	1623	Sir Thomas Posthumus Hoby Sir William Mallory	
Charles I	1625	Sir Thomas Posthumus Hoby Sir William Mallory	
	1626	Sir Thomas Posthumus Hoby Thomas Best	
	1628	Sir Thomas Posthumus Hoby Sir William Mallory	
	1640 April	Sir William Mallory Sir Paul Neile	
	1640	Sir William Mallory John Mallory (The 'Long' Parliament)	
	1645	Ald. Miles Moody Sir Charles Egerton	
Charles I	1646	Sir John Bourchier (vice Miles Moody, deceased)	

Appendix 7 - Members of Parliament for Ripon

Monarch	Date	Returned	Other candidates
Commonwealth		No returns from Ripon to the parliaments of 1653, 1654 or 1656	
	1658-9	Edmund Jenings Jonathan Jenings	
Charles II	1660	Henry Arthington Edmund Jenings	
	1661	Thomas Burwell LL.D Sir John Nicholas	
	1673	Sir Edmund Jenings Alderman (Vice Thomas Burwell deceased)	
	1678	Sir Edmund Jenings Richard Sterne	
	1679	Richard Sterne Christopher Wandesford	
	1680	Richard Sterne Christopher Wandesford	
James II	1685	Gilbert Dolben Sir Edmund Jenings	
	1688	Sir Jonathan Jenings Sir Edward Blackett	Sir Edmund Jenings
William and Mary	1689	Sir Edmund Jenings Sir Jonathan Jenings	
William III	1695	Sir Jonathan Jenings (vice Edmund Jenings deceased) John Aislabie	
	1698	Jonathan Jenings John Aislabie	
	1700	Jonathan Jenings John Aislabie	
	1701	John Aislabie John Sharpe	
	1702	John Sharpe Sir William Hustler	
	1705	John Sharpe John Aislabie	
	1708	John Sharpe John Aislabie	
	1710	John Sharpe John Aislabie	
	1713	John Sharpe John Aislabie	
	1814	John Sharpe (vice John Sharpe)	
George I	1715	John Aislabie Viscount Castlecomer	John Sharpe
	1719	William Aislabie (vice Viscount Castlecomer deceased)	
	1720	John Aislabie Jnr (vice John Aislabie, expelled)	
	1722	William Aislabie John Scrope	
George II	1727	William Aislabie William Aislabie Jnr	
	1728	William Aislabie (vice William Aislabie appointed as Auditor of the Imprest)	
	1734	William Aislabie Thomas Duncome	

Monarch	Date	Returned	Other candidates
George I	1741	William Aislabie Hon Henry Vane	
	1742	Hon Henry Vane	
George II	1747	William Aislabie Sir Charles Vernon	
	1754	William Aislabie Sir Charles Vernon	
George III	1761	William Aislabie William Lawrence	
	1768	William Aislabie Charles Allanson	
	1774	William Aislabie Charles Allanson	
	1775	William Lawrence (vice Charles Allanson deceased)	
	1780	William Aislabie William Lawrence	
	1781	Hon Frederick Robinson (vice William Aislabie, deceased)	
	1784	William Lawrence Hon Frederick Robinson	
	1787	Sir John Goodricke (vice Hon F Robinson, resigned)	
	1789	Sir George Allanson Winn (vice Sir John Goodricke, deceased)	
	1790	William Lawrence Sir George Allanson Winn	
	1796	William Lawrence Sir George Allanson Winn	
	1798	John Heathcote vice Sir G A Winn, (Lord Headley), deceased	
	1798	Sir James Graham vice William Lawrence, deceased	
	1802	John Heathcote Sir James Graham	
	1806	Sir James Graham Lord Headley	
	1807	Hon Frederick John Robinson George Gipps	
	1810	Hon Frederick John Robinson (vice Hon F J Robinson, appt Commissioner of the Admiralty)	
	1812	Hon Frederick John Robinson George Gipps	
	1818	Rt Hon Frederick John Robinson (vice Hon F J Robinson, appt Treasurer of the Navy)	
	1818	Rt Hon Frederick John Robinson George Gipps	
George IV	1820	Rt Hon Frederick John Robinson George Gipps	
	1823	Rt Hon Frederick John Robinson (vice Hon F J Robinson, appt Chancellor of the Exchequer)	

Appendix 7 - Members of Parliament for Ripon

Monarch	Date	Returned	Other candidates
George IV	1826	Rt Hon Frederick John Robinson Lancelot Shadwell	
	1827	Louis Hayes Petit (vice Hon F J Robinson, created Viscount Goderich)	
	1828	Sir Robert Harry Inglis (vice L Shadwell, appt Vice-Chancellor)	
	1829	George Spence QC (Vice Sir R H Inglis, resigned to stand for Oxford University)	
William IV	1830	Louis Hayes Petit George Spence	
	1831	Louis Hayes Petit George Spence	
	1832	Thomas Kitchingman Staveley	
		Joshua Samuel Crompton	Sir James Dalbiac KCB William Markham
	1835	Sir James Dalbiac KCB Thomas Pemberton	Thomas Kitchingman Staveley
Victoria	1837	Thomas Pemberton Sir Edward Burtenshaw Sugden	
	1841	Thomas Pemberton Sir Edward Burtenshaw Sugden	
	1841	Sir George Cockburn GCB (Vice Sir E B Sugden appt Lord Chancellor of Ireland)	
	1843	Thomas B Cusac Smith (vice Thomas Pemberton, resigned)	
	1846	Hon Edwin Lascelles (vice T B C Smith, appt Master of the Rolls for Ireland)	
	1847	Hon Edwin Lascelles Rt Hon Sir James Graham	
	1852	William Beckett Hon Edwin Lascelles	Augustus Newton
	1857	John Ashley Warke John Greenwood	
	1859	John Greenwood John Ashley Warke	Alfred B Richards
	1860	Reginald Arthur Vyner (vice J Warke, deceased)	Frederick Richard Lees
	1865	Sir Charles Wood Robert Kearsley	John Greenwood
	1866	Lord John Hay	
	1868	Lord John Hay	George Allanson Cayley
	1871	Sir Henry Knight Storks	George A Cayley
	1874	Rt Hon Earl de Grey	
	1880	Rt Hon George Joachim Goschem	Francis Darwin

Monarch	Date	Returned	Other candidates
Victoria	1885	William Harker	John Lloyd Wharton
	1886	John Lloyd Wharton (Unionist)	C A C Ponsonby
Edward VII	1906	H F G Lynch (Liberal)	
	1910	Hon. E L Wood (Unionist)	
George V	1925	J W Hills (Conservative)	
	1938	Christopher Yorke (Conservative)	
	1950	Malcolm Stoddart-Scott (Conservative)	
Elizabeth II	1973	David Austick (Liberal)	
	1974	Keith Hampson (Conservative)	
	1983	John Watson (Conservative)i	
	1987	David Curry (Conservative)	

Appendix 8 - Wakemen of Ripon

As listed in the Ripon Millenary page 2.

1400	James Percival		1433	John Pulley
1401	John Lamb		1434	Ralph Ratcliffe
1402	Peter Millbe		1435	William Geldart
1403	William Norton		1436	John Fairborn
1404	Thomas Fountains		1437	Jno Bayne
1405	Randall Backhouse		1437	WWm Wilson
1406	Geoffrey Thorpe		1438	Francis Smith
1407	John Blowmar		1439	Thomas Watson
1408	John Blackburne		1440	Allan Newton
1409	William Trowlope		1441	William Snow
1410	Peter Selby (Gent)		1442	John Wythes (or Wise)
1411	Lawrence Pawl		1443	Adam Spence
1412	Adam Green		1444	Lawrence Rawling
1413	James Hebden (Gent)		1445	Peter Webby
1414	John Davill (Gent)		1445	Jno Freb'die
1415	John Selby		1446	Thomas Porter
1416	Ralph Hanley		1447	John Staveley (Gent)
1417	Peter Allan		1448	Peter Cumberland
1418	William Walby		1449	Jenkin Pratt
1419	Thomas Brook (Gent)		1450	William Fox
1420	Rowland Gill		1451	Ralph Todd
1421	Adam Man (Gent)		1452	Lambert Johnson
1422	Francis Scroop (Gent)		1453	John Stephen
1423	Richard Hebdin (Gent)		1454	William Pulleyn (Gent)
1424	Laurence Dunning		1455	George Pratt
1425	Hierome Blunt		1456	Ralph Clay
1426	Anthony Day		1457	Francis Steel
1426	Jn Snow		1458	John Speed
1427	Abraham Bell		1459	Ralph Tankard
1428	John Digby (Gent)		1460	James Glover
1429	William Single		1461	Peter Robinson
1430	John Bland		1462	John Major
1431	William Bolkend		1463	William Staveley (Gent)
1432	Peter Brough		1464	John Grame

1465	Thomas Hebden (Gent)		1497	Robert Hunter
1466	Peter Jenkins		1498	Robert Leedes (Gent)
1467	Jn Frebodine		1499	Thomas Glewe (Gent)
1467	Wm Leke		1500	John Topliffe
1468	Francis Saunderson		1501	Michael Casson
1469	William Shipton		1502	John Hollmaine
1470	Thomas Snow		1503	Richard Goldsbrough (Gent)
1471	Randall Piggot		1504	John Shearewod
1472	John Whaire		1505	John Bowlande
1473	Ralph Ratcliffe		1506	Stephen Thorpe
1474	Hierome Newby		1506	William Middleton
1475	William Todd		1507	Hugh Stickbuck
1476	Peter Welby		1507	Robert Kettlewell
1477	John Fawcett		1508	Jn (or G) Bellgatt
1478	Thomas Glew (Gent)		1508	John Pansicks
1479	James Hepden (Gent)		1509	Roger De Nunwicke (Gent)
1480	John Ripley		1509	Willm Steele
1481	Peter Benson		1510	John Cooke(Gent)
1482	John Thornton		1511	Wm Batty
1483	James Cundal		1511	Wm Carver
1484	William Thorpe		1512	Rober Holme
1485	John Norton		1512	Wm Wilson
1485	William de Selbie		1513	Simon Plowman (Blowmand)
1487	Roger Harmon		1514	Tho.Bilton (Gen)
1488	Peter Kitchingman		1514	Laurence Langhon
1489	William de Boyte (or Boyes) (Gent)		1515	Henry Sigswick
1490	Renald (or Reginald) Stamth (or Stamworth)		1515	Thomas Fysscher
			1516	Richd Percivell
1491	Christopher Bayliffe		1516	Wm Steele
1492	Marmaduke Burton		1517	John Middleton
1493	Roger (orR) Steele (or Selby)		1518	John Bachus
1494	John Peelgrave		1519	Simon Bateman
1495	Robert Bachus		1519	Wm Brigham
1496	Nicholas Porter		1520	Thomas Gayetsker

159

Appendix 8 - Wakemen of Ripon

1521	Thomas Mankyn		1546	John Walles
1521	Thomas Winpenie		1547	Ralph Horner
1522	Wm Ledes		1547	Ralph Rippley alias Dixon
1522	Robert Barron		1548	James Fletcher
1523	Wm Hebden (Gent)		1549	Robert Harrison
1523	Richrd Gowthart		1550	William Scott
1524	Thos Halle		1551	John Thornton
1524	Edmond Warde		1552	Willm Wheatley
1525	Wm Horner		1553	John Hollmes
1525	James Clarke		1554	Hugh Foxe
1526	John Dicson		1555	Willm Tompson
1526	Abraham Cumberland		1556	John Smith (Vintner)
1527	Robt Playne		1557	Edmond Lockley
1527	Thos Kettlewell		1558	Willm Rener (or Rayner)
1528	Lawrence Hodgson		1559	Thomas Rigg
1529	Richard Terrie		1560	Willm Smithe
1530	Rowland Wilson		1561	Robert Ripplay
1531	Thomas Staveley (Gent)		1562	Christopher Dalle (or Dale)
1532	Richard Bell		1563	John Sweetinge
1533	William Gentleman		1564	Willm Harrison
1534	William Kettlewell		1565	Thomas Ripplay
1535	John Johnson		1566	Richard Mounton (or Monkton)
1535	Wm Steele		1567	John Rigg
1536	Thomas Benson		1568	Emerie Coots (or Coates)
1536	Matt Snow		1569	Robert Kettlewell
1537	Anthony Vickerby		1570	Thomas Swyers (or SawyersO
1538	Ralph Cooke		1571	John Hodgson
1539	Robert Ripplay		1572	Thomas Newell
1540	John Middleton		1573	Christopher Thornton
1541	George Younge		1574	Jeffrey Medcalf
1542	Christopher Darnbrough		1575	George Battie
1543	Ralph Bell		1576	Thomas Hebdin
1544	Henry Atkinson		1577	Christopher Gaines
1545	Matthew Snowe		1578	William Watson

1579	John Millner
1580	Thomas Grainge
1581	John Dobbie
1582	Henry Lockie
1583	Vincent Metcalfe
1583	Thomas Ripley
1584	Willm Wray
1585	Anthony Holmes
1586	Ant. Vickerby (or Uckerbie)
1587	Roger Holmes
1588	Christopher Ffranke
1589	Richard Cooke
1590	Ralph Hutchinson (Tanner)
1591	Richard Reyner
1592	Thomas Dowgill
1593	Thomas Barber
1594	William Fawcett
1595	Simon Browne
1596	Thomas Harland
1597	John Middleton (Gent)
1598	Henry Singleton (Mercer)
1599	Francis Healey
1599	Simon Askewe
1600	Simon Askewe (or Ayscough)
1601	John Greene
1602	Thomas Wardropyer
1603	Thomas Cundall (Tanner)
1604 to June 26th	Hugh Ripley

Appendix 9 - Picture credits

Every effort has been made to trace copyright holders - we apologise for any not acknowledged - this will be corrected in future reprints.

Page	Acknowledge	Other details
20;	Ashworth, Canon James	Ripon Cathedral
84;	*Bonneys Cathedrals*	Revd H D Cust Nunn
5	Bradley, Tom	*Yorkshire Weekly Post 1891*
76;	Brett, Russell	
35; 47a; 48b; 107; 111;	Carroll, Brian	
91;	Chapman, Mrs Bessie	
98;	Crew, Mrs Jennifer	
96;	Cross, Miss M	In Rogers, P W
2 top,	Curtis, Andrew	
78;	Forth, Maurice	
	Fremantle, Dean W H	
8; 9; 11; 13;	Gent, Thos.	*History of Ripon (1733)*
67; 115;	Gott, Jim	From Kelvin Gott collection
2	Griffiths, Mike	
55;	Hague, J W	From the D V Beeken collection
	Hardaker, Mrs Avril	
102;	Harrison, John	
51; 127	Harrogate Borough Council	David Rhodes & Andrew Donaldson
3; 90;	Harrogate Museum	
63;	*Historic Ripon*	
79;	*Illustrated London News*	
68c; 103;	Jackson, George	
	Jones, W D,.	*Prosperity Robinson,* (Macmillan, London, 1967).
	Kellett, Arnold	
83; 126;	Lambie, Robert	
	Lukis, Revd W C	
124;	Oakenfull, Michael	
12;	Rands, Angus	
106	Richards, Mark and Catherine	
24; 38; 101b; 110;	Ripon Cathedral	
65; 68a;	Ripon City Council	& Fossick Collection
72[a];	*Ripon Record*	Ripon Civic Society
	Ripon in Old Picture Postcards	Ripon Civic Society

162

Page	Acknowledge	Other details
28;	Ripon Town Trail	Ripon Civic Society
68b; 70; 74c;	Ripon Community History Collection	
Ack page; 4; 52; 53; 81; 86b; 128; 129; 131;	*Ripon Gazette*	
114;	Ripon House resident	
101a;	Ripon Local Studies Centre	Mike Younge
14; 39; 43a; 64; 100;	*Ripon Millenary Record*	
54;	Ripon Motor Boat Club	
	Ripon Museum Trust	
116;	Robson, Bill	
57;	Rosher, Joan	
36;	Senior, John	
	Story of Ripon Minster	Lucius Smith
99a;	*Story of Skellfield School 1877 1927*	(Skellfield School).
68d;	*Jepson Story*	Percival Smith
72b;	Stride, Alan	
17;	Tinsley, Mrs	
49;	Unicorn Hotel	
85;	Waite, Roy	
26;	Walbran, J R	Guide to Ripon
33; 48a; 125;	*Wakeman Magazine*	
7; 9; 16; 21; 29; 31; 37; 40; 43b; 45; 82; 89; 99b; 107; 108; 113; 118;	Watson, Keith	
64; 65;	Williamson, T & R	
68c;	Wimpress, John and Susie	
22;	York Archaeological Trust	Dr Richard Hall
94;	Yorkshire Archaeological Society	

Index

Look under the specific name or subject. Bridges, Mills and Schools are, however, grouped under those headings. Illustrations are shown on pages with figures in bold.

agriculture, regulations, 60
Ailcey Hill, 2, 4, **4**
Aislabie, John, 12, 59
Aislabie, William, 13
Aismunderby, 48
Alchfrid, prince, 20, 21, 22
Alfred, king, 25
Alice in Wonderland, see Carroll, Lewis
Allanson, Elizabeth, 18
Alma bridge and weir, **46**
almshouses, 28-32
apple distribution, 84
Appleton's sausages, 107
Aram, Eugene, 106
archaeology, 2-4
Archbishops of York, and Ripon, 6-7, 8-9, 10, 12, 21, 37, 38, 42, 113
see also under the names of individual archbishops
Army camp, 51, 76, 122-3, **122, 123**
Ashworth, Canon I.G.B., **20**
Aslin, Robert, lace merchant, 65
Assembly Rooms (Town Hall), 92
Athelstan, king, 6, 25
Atrium Leisure Club, 73, 93

bailiffs, duties, 36, 37
Baldersby Park, 99

Balfour, Neil, 104
bands, 94-5, **94**
Baring-Gould, Revd. Sabine, 108
Barnardo's schools, 103
Baronway, **48**, 49
bastardy, 87
bathing facilities, 72, 73
Bede, 5, 20
bedern and Bedern Bank, 39
beggars, 86
Bellman, 16, **16**, 115
bells, curfew, 82-3
Beverley, 26
Bishopton, schools at, 97
see also mills
bishops of Ripon, list, 154/2
Black Bull Inn, 50
Blore, Edward, 44
bobbin manufacture, 65
Bondgate, 57, 61
Bone, Florence, 108
bone house, **27**
bowling, 93
Boroughbridge, 6, 49, 54
Boxing Day Procession, 86, **86**
Bradford, Barbara Taylor, 108
Bradley, Marmaduke, abbot, 32, 42
breweries, 65
bridges, 56-9
  Alma bridge, **46**
  Archer bridge, 59
  Bishopton bridge, 57
  Bondgate bridge, 56, 57
  Bondgate Green bridge, 58
  Borrage bridge, 57
  Chain bridge, 58, 59
  Hewick bridge, 56-7

New bridge, 58
North bridge, 46, 48, 56
Rustic bridge, **58**, 59
Bromflet family, woodcarvers, 40-1
Brontë, Charlotte, 108
Buck, Samuel and Nathaniel, **57**
buckle-making, 64, **65**
burgages, 6-7, 46
burgesses, 46-7
burials, Ailcey Hill, 4
Burton, Mrs Ada, 78, **78**
Butler, Samuel, theatre company, 90, **90**

cabmen's shelter, 124-5, **124**
canal, 54-5, **54, 55**
Candlemas, 83, **83**
cannon, Crimean War, **117**
Capper Hall, 10
Carpenter, Bishop William Boyd, 110
Carroll, Lewis, **43**, 44, 90, 97, 106, **106**
cathedral, **37, 45**
  as market, 7
  building, as minster, 26, 33-4, **33, 34, 35**
  building, 15th-16th centuries, 40-1, **42**
  during Civil War, 10
  Chapter's jurisdiction, 36
  collapses, 40, 42
  restorations, 44
  new diocese, 43
Cathedral Choir School, 103
cattle trade, 12, 18-19, 60
cattlegates, 60

Celts in Ripon, 20-1
Chambers, Sir William, 105
chantry chapels, 28, 32, 42
chapels:
    medieval, 38
    St. Anthony, 56
    St. Sitha, 56
    see also Lady Chapel;
    St. Anne's; St. John's;
    St. Mary Magdalen's
chapter house, bone store, **27**
Charles, Prince of Wales, **126**
charters:
    not from Alfred, 25
    1108, 6, 36, 37
    1228, 25
    1604, 10, 18
    1688, 12
cholera, 75
Church Institute, 93
churches in Ripon:
    All Hallows, 38
    Holy Trinity, 118, **118**
    Lady Kirk, 38
    *see also chapels and under the
    names of other denominations*
cinemas, 92, **92**
City Club, 98
civic pride, **11**, 72-9
Civil War, 10
Clock Tower, 119, **119**
cloth making, 10, 12, 62
coaching inns, 50
coal imports, 54
Cocoa House tokens, 86, **86**
College of Ripon and York St.
    John, 100, **100**

collegiate church (Ripon Minster),
    26, 42
Collier, Alice, 101
Company of Drapers, Dyers,
    Apothecaries, and Barber-
    Surgeons, 61
comprehensive education, 102
Congregational chapel, 119, **119**
constabularies, township divisions,
    47, 88
Corbridge, Archbishop Thomas, 39
cottages, 46, 60-1
cotton mills, 70
courthouse, **36**, 116-17, **116**
cricket, 93
Crimean War, **117**
Crompton, Colonel Rookes Evelyn
    Bell, 109
crosses, sanctuary, 26, **26**
Crudd, Tom, **49**
crypt (cathedral), 3, **21**, 21, 22,
    27-8, **27, 84**
curfew bells, 82-3
Cuthbert, Saint, 20-1, 26

daffodil banks, **48**
Danes, in Ripon, 25
Davill's Bakery, 86
Deanery, Old, **39**
Defoe, Daniel, quoted, 13, 49
Diocese, Ripon, new, 43
Dissenters, 119-20
Dodgson, Canon Charles, 44
Dodgson, Charles Lutwidge, *see*
    Carroll, Lewis
Domesday Survey, 26-7, 67

Eadhead, Bishop of Ripon, 24
Eadred, king, 26
Eata, Abbot of Melrose, 20, 21
Econ Engineering, 127
Eddius Stephanus, 5, 23, 96
education, 96-103
electricity supply, 76
Elizabeth II, Queen, **128**, 129, **129**
Elliott, John, 105
Elmcroft, 74
employment, 60-71
enclosure, 60
evacuees, World War II, 102
excursions to Ripon, 121

fairs and feasts, 6, 10, 12
Fairy Steps, **58**, 59
farming, regulations, 60
Farrer, William, bookseller, 76
feasts and fairs, 6, 10, 12
Fiennes, Celia, quoted, 9, 56-7
Fisher Green, 76
flax mill, 70
floods, 56, 57, 72-3
football, 94
fords, 46, 57
foundries, 66-7
fountain, Severs, **50**
Fountains Abbey, 42, 62
    processions to, 86, **86**
Fremantle, Dean Wm Robert, 73
fulling, 61, 62, 69
Furness, Sir Christopher, 74

Gallows Hill, 9
Garnett, burlers and menders, 65
Garnett, Elizabeth, 108-9
gazebo, **51**

165

Index

Gent, Thomas, illustrations, **8, 13**
geology, 3, 5
Gibson, William, 12
glaciers, 3, 5
golf, 93
Gordon, Father, Bishop of Leeds, 119
de Gray, Archbishop Walter, 6, 34, 38
de Greenfield, Archbishop William, 7
guilds, 61
gun, Crimean War, **117**

Hall, Dr Richard, 3, 22
Hall, Philip, Store, 125
hangings, 9
Hansom, Joseph, 119
Harrogate District, 112
'Harrying of the North', 26-7
Hassell, George, 90
Hawksmoor, Nicholas, 12
hearth tax, 47, **47**
Hemsworth, William, 17
Henry I, 6
Henry VI, 8
Herstretegate, 48
Hexham, 21, 23
High Cleugh dam, 68, 70, 72
holiday excursions to Ripon, 121
Holy Trinity Church, 118, **118**
Hooke, Dean Richard, 32
Hornblower, 14-15, **14**, 82, **82**, 131, **131**
horns, 11, 14-16, **14, 64**
horse racing, 80-1, **80**

Horsefair, 12, 18
horses, trade in, 12, 18
hospitals, 112
    medieval, 28
hotels and inns, 50
House of Correction, **112**, 113
housewarmings, 78
housing, 10, 12, 51
Hrype tribe, 5
Hugh Ripley Hall, 70

Ibbetson, Julius Caesar, artist, **15**
industrial estate, 127
Ingram, J., foundry, 66-7
inns, 50

Jacob, Naomi, 99, 107, **107**
James I, 10, 42, 63
James II, 10, 12
Jennings, Sir Edmund, 47
Jepson, Zacarias, 98, 104
Jepson's Hospital and School, **68**, 97, 98, **98**
Jones, Professor G.R.J., 46

Kean, Edmund, 90
Kearsley foundry, 66-7, **66**, 120
Kilvington, Thomas, 118
King, Daniel, artist, **33**
Knaresborough, 8, 48, 106

lace making, 22, 64-5
Lady Chapel (cathedral), 40
Lady Kirk, 38
lamps, **76**, 78
Lark Hill, 112
Lavender Alley, 9

Laver (river), 5
    bridges, 57, 59
Lawrence, Sophia, 18, 61
leather making, 62
Leeds Metropolitan University, 99
Leland, John, 12, 48, 56, 62-3
Leper Chapel, *see* Saint Mary Magdalen's Chapel
Levick, Canon, 114
Liberty of Ripon, 21, 25, 37, 42
libraries, public, 93
Liddell, Dean Henry, 97, 106
lighting, street, 76, **76**
livestock trade, 12, 18-19
Longley, Bishop (later Archbishop) Charles Thomas, 43, 110, **110**, 112
Lukis, Revd W.C., 18

Macfadyen, Neil, 44
magistrates' court (former), 93
Maiden's Bower, 92
Mallorie, Sir John, 10
maltsters, 65
maps, *see* Ripon: maps
Markenfield, Thomas, 9
market cross, 9, **13**
    see also obelisk
market square, 8-9, 12-13, 18-19, **19**, 77
    development, 125, 126, **127**
    table of facts on, 143-4
Marketstead ward, 62
markets in Ripon, 6, 7, 9
Masham, 6
Mason, George, 32
Mauleverer, Sir Thomas, 10

166

mayor and corporation, **11**;
    duties, 18
mayors:
    'seeking the mayor' custom, 78
    list, 147-51
maze, 92
Mechanics' Institute, 77, 93
medical facilities, 112
Members of Parliament, list, 153-7
messuages, 46, 60-1, 62
Methodists, 120
Methuen, Dean John, 130, **130**
military, in Ripon, *see* army camp
mill race, 68-9, 72; map, **71**
mills, 67-71; map, **70-1**
    Bishopton mill, 62, 70, **70**, 76
    Byemill, 67
    Cobham's steam mill, 69
    Duck Hill mill, 67, 68, **68**, 70, 72
    High mill (West mill), **68**, 69, 70
    Low mill (East mill), **46**, 67, **67**
    New mill, 69
    Union mill, 69, **69**
Milner, Mary, 83
Minster, 26
    re-establishment, 42
    loss of power, 88
misericords, 40-1, **40, 43,** 44
monasteries, 20-5
    to Minster, 26
    land for, 60
Montgomery, Field Marshal Bernard, Viscount, 125
Moody, Dr C.H., 95

Moorman, Bishop John, 110
Morris dancers, **85**
Mountain, James, 50
mummers, 85, **85**
museums, 17, 74, 93
music, 94-5
Mylchreest, Mr and Mrs, 103
mystery plays, 85

Newby Park tragedy, 72-3
Nicholls, Revd Arthur Bell, 108
Nonconformists, 119-20
North Grange, 60
North Road Auction Mart, 19
North Stainley, 60
Norton, Richard, 9

obelisk, **9,** 12-13, **13, 15**
Old Deanery, **39**
Old Hall, Allhallowgate, 113
Oldfield, Bruce, 109
Oliver, Alan, hornblower, 131, **131**
opera, 95
Opera House, 90, 92
Owen, Dean Charles Mansfield, **125**
Owen, Wilfred, 107, **107**

Packer, Bishop John, 43, 130
Palace, Bishop's, **43**
Pankhurst, Amelia, 124
paper making, 70, 89
parish, Ripon, 36
Pateley Bridge, 49
peculiar, Ripon, 36, 37
Peter of Blois, Canon, 34
photography, 95

pinfolds (pounds), 12, 61
Pipe Roll 1194, 6, 47
plague, 12, 40
Plantagenet, Archbishop Geoffrey, 33-4
policing, 115-17
Poll Tax 1379, 47, 62
pont l'Eveque, Bishop Roger, 33
poor, 88, 113, 120-2
Poor Law Museum, 93, **113,** 114
poorhouse, 113, **113**
postal service, 76-7
pounds (pinfolds), 12, 61
poverty, *see* poor
prebends, 26, 35, 39, 86
    houses, map, **35**
Primitive Methodists, 120
Prison and Police Museum, 93
prisons, 115, 116-17
public libraries, 93
punishments, 9, 10, 36, 38-9
Puritans in Ripon, 10

Quarry Moor, 3, 60-1
Quo Warranto hearings, 25

racing, horse, 80-1, **80**
railways, 51, 54, 55, **55,** 77
Ratcliffe, Dorothy Una, 108
Rawley, Marmaduke, 12
recorder, office of , 10, 112
Residence, The, **44**
Richardson, Sir Albert, 44
Ripley, Hugh, 10, 17
Ripon, 1st Marquis of, *see* Robinson, George Frederick Samuel

Index

Ripon:
   archaeology, 3
   as borough, 6, 47
   as city, 112
   death rate 1894-5, 121
   incorporation, 10
   maps, **8, 44, 48, 70-1, 111**;
   list of, 141
   origin, 20
   origin of name, 5
   parish and peculiar, 36
   population, 47, 51
   prospects of, **8, 57**
   regeneration, 126-7
   streets, 46-7; list, 142
   wards, 47; map, **47**
Ripon City Band, 94-5, **94**
Ripon City Partnership, 131
Ripon College (1949 version), 102
Ripon Diocese, creation, 112
Ripon Hall, Oxford, 100
Ripon jewel, **38**
Ripon Museum Trust, 93
Ripon Park, 60
Ripon peculiar, 36, 37
Ripon Prison and Police Museum, 117
Ripon Training College, 99, **99**, 100, **100**
Ripon Union (Poor Law), 113
'Riponians' concert party, **123**
Rising of the North 1569, 9
rivers, 72-3
   see also Laver; Skell; Ure
roads, 49
   by-pass, 52-3, **52-3**

Robinson, Frederick John, 1st Earl of Ripon, **104**
Robinson, George Frederick Samuel, 1st Marquis of Ripon, 18, 74, 97, 104, 119
Roger of Bishopsbridge, Archbishop of York, 27
Roman Catholicism, 101, 118-19
Romans in Ripon, 3-4, 22, 46
rope-walks, 70
Rowe, Sebastian, 32
Royal Engineers, 123
rugby football, 94

saddletree-making, 65, **65**
St. Anne's Hospital and Chapel, 28, **28, 29**, 38
St. John's Hospital and Chapel, 28, 30-1, **30**, 38, 96
St. Mary Magdalen's Chapel, 4, 28-9, 31-2, **31**, 38
St. Wilfrid's Roman Catholic Church, 119
St. Wilfrid's well, 89, **89**
saints, *see under their own names*
Salvation Army, 120
sanctuary, right of, 26;
   crosses, 26, **26**
schools, 31, 96-103
   Barnardo's Schools, 103
   Coltsgate Hill School, 102, **102**
   Greystone Primary School, 101
   High School, 99
   Jepson's School, 97, 98, **98**

   National Schools, 31, 97, **101**, 101
   Mr Pickersgill's School, 97
   Ripon Girls' High School, 99, **99**
   Ripon Grammar School, 96-7, **96**
   Ripon Industrial Home for Girls, 101, **101**
   St. Wilfrid's Roman Catholic School, 101
   Skellfield School, 99, **99**
   Wesleyan School, 101, **102**
   Westholme Girls' School, 103, **103**
   others, 101-2
Scots, as invaders, 34
Scott, Sir Gilbert, **43**, 44
Scune, Christopher, 41
Select Vestry, 87, 88; staves, **87**
setting the watch, 14-15, **14**
Severs Fountain, **50**
sewers, 75-6
Sharow Cross, **26**
sheep, 12, 60
sheriff, duties, 37
shops, 125
Sigma Antiques, 92
sin eaters, 83
Single Regeneration Scheme, 126, **126**
Skell (river), 5, **58**
   bridges, 57, **58**, 59
Skellgate, 48
Skellgate Ward, 62
slums, 75, 121
Smeaton, John, 54

Smith, Professor Charles Piazzi, **108,** 109
spa, decline, 122
Spa Baths, 74-5, **74-5**
Spa Gardens, **74**
Spa Hotel (Fountains Hotel), 74-5, 76
spur-making, 63-4, **63**
Stanwick Prebend, 35
station, railway, 55
staves, Select Vestry, 87, **87**
Stead, Samuel, 74
stocks, 9
Stonebridgegate (Ward), 48, 62
Stubbs, Thomas, **46**
Stubbs, Bishop William, 109
Studley Royal, 76, 79
    political role, 88, 104
suffragettes, 124
swimming, **72,** 73
sword, Iron Age, 3, **3**
Sykes, Paul, 104

tanning, 62
Taylor, Maurice, **126**
telephones, 77
temperance movement, 124
tennis, 93
Terry, John, spurrier, 63, **65**
theatre, 90-1, **90-1**
Thomas, Archbishop of York, 27
Thomas II, Archbishop of York, 30
Thornborough, **2,** 3
Thorpe Prebend, 35-6
Thorpe Prebend House, 93
Thurstan, Archbishop of York, 6, 31
tithes, 85
tollbooth, 9
tolls, 16-17
Torrington, John Byng, Viscount, 15
Town Hall (and Assembly Rooms), 18, 92
Towne Book 1598, 9, 60
Treaty of Ripon, 42
turnpike roads, 49

Unicorn Inn, **49,** 50
university, proposed for Ripon, 99
Ure (river), 5, 50-1, 72, **72;** map, **5**
Ure Navigation Canal, logo, **54**

vagrants, 114
varnish making, 66, **66**
Vestry, Select, *see* Select Vestry
Victoria, Queen, diamond jubilee, **119**
Victoria Hall, 90, 92

Wakeman's House, 17, **17,** 93
wakemen, 14-15, **14;** list, 160-3
Walker, Thomas, lace merchant, 65
water mills, *see* mills
Water Skellgate, 68, **68**
water supply, 72, 73, 123
Wesleyans, *see* Methodists
West Riding Constabulary, 116, 117
Westgate Ward, 62
wife sales, 86-7
Wilfra tarts, 78, **78**
Wilfrid, Saint, 6, 21-5, **24,** 96
    monastery, 21-2
    elevation, 33, 34
    shrine destroyed, 42
    feasts, 79, 81
    statue, **6**
    St. Wilfrid Procession, **78,** 79, **79,** 81, **81**
Wilkinson, Walter, quoted, 19
Williamson, Daniel, varnish maker, 66
Williamson, T. and R., and Jepson's School, 98
Willibrord, St., 96
witchcraft, 83
Wolseley Centers, 127
woodcarving, in Cathedral, 40-1, **40, 41**
work, 60-71
workhouse 113, **113,** 114, **114,** 120
Wyatt, James, 18

'Year's mind' prayers, 83